BLACKTAIL
TROPHY TACTICS *II*

Boyd Iverson

Photo credit for Front Cover of paperback edition: Chuck Bartlett
Photo credit for Back Cover of paperback edition: Jerry Gowins, Jr.

Photo credit for Front Cover of hardbound editon: Jerry Gowins, Jr.

Blacktail Trophy Tactics II
Copyright © 1999 by Boyd Iverson
ISBN 0-9630405-1-0 (paperback edition)
ISBN 0-9630405-2-9 (hardbound edition)

Library of Congress Cataloging-in-Publication Data
Iverson, Boyd.
    Blacktail trophy tactics II / author, Boyd Iverson
       p.   cm.
    ISBN 0-9630405-1-0 (pbk.)
    1. Blacktail deer hunting. I. Title. II. Title: Blacktail trophy tactics 2. III.
    Title: Blacktail trophy tactics two.
    SK301.I842 1999
    799.2'7653--dc21
    99-30406
    CIP

Printed in Korea.

Dedication

This book is dedicated to all of the great people out there who encouraged me on my first book. I had planned on only writing one book on blacktail deer hunting but at the request of all of you who kept asking me "when are you going to write your next book?" I decided that I would do a second.

I have analyzed and have had readers critique my first book and I see where I can make some of the chapters more specific and more helpful. A few chapters remain unchanged, those that I was unable to improve, while other chapters have many subtle but significant additions. I've made major revisions in some chapters, and several are completely new with entirely new information. Those of you who studied my first book will be able to note the various refinements and I hope that you will enjoy my second book as much or even more than the first.

Thanks to all of you who have sent photos of the bucks you have taken with the help of my first book. I enjoy them greatly and keep all of the photos in a book which I take to seminars. I've also included a section of readers' photos in this new book for your enjoyment.

To those who wonder if I have taken any Boone and Crockett bucks since I wrote my first book, the answer is no, but by the letters and phone calls I've received, several of you have. So Congratulations!! In fact Bobby McClory the young boy whose picture was in my first book, took a very nice Boone and Crockett buck a few years later. The photo of Bobby and his buck is in my "Readers Photos" section.

I've taken some good bucks and have had a couple of chances at great bucks but made the wrong move at the wrong time. The area I studied for years, which supplied the basis for my first book, has changed and does not attract the number of trophy bucks it did for so many years.

Nearby logging, increased hunting pressure, and the changes associated with the natural succession and takeover of less desirable plants, has limited the area's productiveness.

I refused to accept this fact for several years and continued to spend my time there and relive all of my old hunts and memories, but I finally accepted the fact that, that was all there was, old memories!

I shot my last large buck at my special spot in 1989 and took my final buck from this area on the last day of the 1993 hunting season. He was an old buck with average head gear but the fun of taking him in my old spot remains unequaled.

So as I had done over 14 years ago, when I first started my search for a Boone and Crockett Blacktail, I have begun my quest again. My search for new locations has prompted me to rethink what it took to discover a quality blacktail hot spot in the first place and therefore rehash the techniques and information which I presented in my original book.

The blacktail deer itself has changed little during this time, except possibly to become even more secretive and nocturnal, but some of the new techniques, information and equipment are worth exploring further.

My last large buck at my special spot 1989. B & C score: 123

This was an old buck but he didn't put much effort into head gear. I shot him the last 10 to 15 minutes, on the last day of the deer season in 1993, at my special spot.

When we think that we know it all or are unwilling to try and experiment with new ideas or concepts, it's time that we hung up our bows or guns and spent our time wasting away in some rocking chair watching soap operas.

I would certainly hope that we all have better things to do and one of those things would be to continue to try to figure out how to more successfully outsmart this evasive quarry.

If this book is of benefit to you, I would appreciate knowing about it and would enjoy hearing about your hunting experiences or seeing photos of any bucks you take.

THE HUNT CONTINUES!

C&G Bartlett Photography
Nature & Wildlife

(425) 776-9695
19118-24th. Ave. W.
Lynnwood, WA 98036

All of the fantastic, live, blacktail photographs, including the front cover photo used in my book, except those marked otherwise, were taken by Chuck and Grace Bartlett.

Blacktail photos are one of, if not, the hardest of the deer species to obtain, and Chuck and Grace have an amazing collection of beautiful photographs!

Chuck and Grace Bartlett were born and raised in Eastern Oregon but have lived in Western Washington for the past 37 years. They are both avid hunters and also, obviously, great photographers. Their observation and insight into blacktail deer behavior is unequalled. They have been able to not only witness, but also photograph blacktail behavior seldom seen by the average hunter or outdoors person. Through their photography they are able to capture and share with others some of what they have discovered.

As professional wildlife photographers, blacktail deer are one of the main species they pursue, and for the past 10 years this pursuit has taken up a major portion of their time.

During their long term interaction with the animals which they photograph, some of the animals have actually grown so accustomed to their presence that they are accepted and the animals will actually allow them to be part of their daily activities. This has allowed them to observe blacktail behavior seldom seen and rarely photographed by others.

These are not photos taken on a game preserve, but are actually all wild, free ranging, animals, living in their natural habitat. Some of the animals photographed have been killed during hunting season, some have been poached and others have survived for several years, becoming a great resource for study and photography. Other animals have allowed the Bartletts only a quick glimpse or photograph and then never been seen again.

Obtaining quality blacktail deer photographs is very difficult, since typically they live in heavy poorly lit cover. The weather is ever changing, rain is a constant companion and the animals are most active either early or late, when the amount of available light is very scarce.

Taking pictures of mature blacktails is actually even harder than hunting them, because not only do you have to locate the animals, you have to see them during a time when there is sufficient light to obtain a quality photograph.

I for one am very appreciative of what they have accomplished and it is an honor for me to be able to use their photographs in my book about blacktail deer. The deer which I have also studied and love so much.

What Ansel Adams was to black and white photography the Bartletts are to blacktail photography!

If you ever want any beautiful photographs of blacktail bucks or other quality outdoor photography, for professional use or personal enjoyment, give them a call.

Readers' Comments

Please look also at the section containing photos of readers bucks.

Here are some of the quotes which have been received on my original book:

"Your book "Blacktail Trophy Tactics" is the best single book I have ever read on hunting. It is absolutely incredible. It has resulted in my seeing more game than ever before. There simply is no other book like it with its wealth of information and careful attention to detail." S.L.

"I was telling my friend that I should use this book as a required, annual personal refresher course... right along with Jack O'Connor's, "The Art of Big Game Hunting." Your chapters on scents and tree stands were particularly interesting to me...I just want to let you know that the effort that you put into preparing this informative, well-written book is appreciated." R.M.

"It was the third day into the Western Oregon buck hunt. Mom loaned me your book to read before the next morning's hunt. I opened the book and didn't put it down again until I had read every line, cover to cover. I used your ideas and techniques and they worked. I shot a 120+ buck." B.H.

"I'm writing to tell you how much I enjoyed your book. I borrowed this book from a friend who borrowed it from his friend. Needless to say we have been squabbling over it for more than a week now. You've certainly done your homework." A.M.

"This is a letter for my son J.C.. He has gained more knowledge and gotten more enjoyment from your Book than any of the others he has read. Thank you."

"After reading your book I realized that somewhere in my subconscious many of the principles you state and observations you make I already knew to be true. I am attempting to tell you that your book opened my mind and my eyes to be even more observant. I will make it required pre-season reading every year, and it will also help me get closer in the off-season for photography." J.W.

"The last two years I shot a blacktail buck, a mule deer buck and a pronghorn antelope. In all of these hunts, aspects of your book helped me in my success." C.H.

"Your book makes excellent points about deer hunting in general as well as particular steps for blacktail. It will be a valuable addition to my library of hunting books. It won't go into the bookcase, however, it will find a home on the shelf above my computer alongside Dwight's "Bowhunting for Mule Deer" and Leonard Rue's "Deer of North America…" R.B.

"Your book has changed the way I think in terms of analyzing the areas I hunt and the way I approach hunting altogether! The information in your book has clarified many of the things I have seen over the years but never fully realized." M.S.

"Thanks for sharing your years of experience in blacktail deer hunting. It's given me more knowledge and confidence in my hunting." B.H.

"I am 61 and have hunted blacktails since I was 19 and feel there's no greater challenge. I'm really looking forward to reading your book and hope to apply some of your techniques to my hunting efforts." D.P. This is D.P's next note after reading my book. "I have just finished your book and want you to know what a marvelous contribution your work is to hunting in general and blacktail hunters specifically." D.P.

"I would like to request two autographed copies of "Blacktail Trophy Tactics" I have already purchased one myself and read it cover to cover. I was so impressed that I plan to buy two for my hunting buddies. This is really a good technical book for blacktails. Thank-you" J.G.

"Enclosed is a check for another copy of "Blacktail Trophy Tactics". I enjoyed it so much, I would like a copy to give to my brother". K.G.

"Thanks for a great book and a lot of help. Those bucks in your book are a testament to your skill. Thanks again and good luck." T.P.

"Just wanted to say "Thanks." I started hunting 4 years ago and have from day one been trying to learn as much as I can. I became "field wise" enough to put venison on the table but never more than a "forkie" year after year. Then I read your book once, then twice, then three times. It was like a light went on in my head. You put together all the pieces of the blacktail habit that I observed and made it MAKE SENSE. Plus other tactics and observations, that would have taken me years to develop. I tried to turn my buddies onto your book but what I got was "You can not learn deer hunting from a book" and then laughter. During the season I passed on several legal bucks and finally took a monster 3 x 3. P.S. My buddies are no longer laughing. A few even have asked to borrow my (your) book. I GAVE THEM YOUR ADDRESS. THANK-YOU, THANK-YOU, THANK-YOU". J.R.

Contents

Foreword

Most American hunters don't realize it, but the blacktail deer of the west coast offers the toughest challenge of all the deer subspecies on the continent. Because most hunters live in the east, midwest, and south, whitetails are their exclusive quarry. In the vastness of the west, mule deer generate the most interest. But to the residents who hunt the very western fringes of the country from California up to Alaska, the blacktail is king.

He lives in an environment that makes most hunters think twice before entering. Picture a dense, often soggy forest that has underbrush so thick that you can't see much more than few yards, coupled with downed, slippery logs that crisscross the forest floor like pick-up sticks, and vegetation that more often than not is armed with thorns and needles, and you'll have some concept of blacktail country.

But a mere description in words can't convey the incredible difficulty in getting around these unique western forests. So it's no surprise that many hunters shun the blacktail's domain and instead hunt the more arid lands in the east, seeking the muley that dwells in a more hospitable environment. This is an interesting enigma, since the large majority of hunters along the west coast live within the blacktail's range, but are perfectly willing to drive several hundred miles for easier game to hunt.

But Boyd Iverson, unlike many hunters, became so enamored with the blacktail and its rugged home, that he elected to challenge the blacktail on his own terms, under quite possibly the worst conditions on the continent. Boyd learned at a young age how to outsmart these deer in their tough turf. Since his first buck at age 12, almost 40 years ago, he has taken an incredible number of impressive trophies. He's accomplished this remarkable feat by observing blacktails intently, learning their habits, behavior patterns, and developing strategies that work.

This book includes a lifetime of information that Boyd gathered in the woods. He describes the techniques that are most successful, and teaches you how to get around in the thick forests. Chapters on recovering wounded animals, ethics, the effects of the moon, and how to find your way around in the woods are just some of the new things you'll learn in this second edition. Other chapters in the first edition have been expanded, offering brand new information. If you have the first edition, be smart and read this one, too.

Boyd Iverson does a masterful job of presenting the ins and outs of hunting blacktails, from the very basic to the most advanced strategies. This book is a must if you intend to step into the blacktail's domain. This savvy deer has a way of outsmarting most hunters. Do yourself a favor and even the odds in your favor. Read this book.

Jim Zumbo, Hunting Editor
OUTDOOR LIFE Magazine

Chapter 1

In My Book He's Still Number One

For those of you who have attempted to match wits with the blacktail deer, this book needs no introduction, but to those who have never had the frustration of being out-smarted by a wise, old, blacktail buck the following will suffice.

As a point of trivia, until recently it was believed that blacktail deer evolved from mule deer. Now it seems that there is strong genetic evidence to suggest that mule deer actually evolved from blacktails. Actually all of us, dyed in the wool blacktail hunters, have known this all along, we just didn't want to hurt any of our mule deer hunting friends' feelings!

I've done some, out of state mule deer hunting in the past few years and I find that many of the smart, old, "open cover," mule deer are acting more like "cover hugging" blacktails, rather than "jump, run, and look back," mule deer. Maybe the blacktail genetic survival instincts are resurfacing.

The blacktail deer is not the lover of wide open spaces like the mule deer, nor is he an animal of habit and routine like the whitetail. The blacktail is a browser and prefers brush-filled hillsides adjacent to more open areas, which supply his dietary needs. Older bucks, especially, operate in a small area, are inconsistent in their habits, do not expose themselves needlessly and, are many times, nocturnal.

Other than the few days a year, when he loses some of his caution during the rut, a blacktail buck is one of the wariest animals a hunter can pursue. But he is also a very available animal. The largest bucks which I have taken, and many of the largest bucks in the record books, were taken within a half hour, to an hour and a half of major cities.

There are migratory blacktails in several areas of Oregon and California but the typical coastal or low elevation blacktail buck will grow up and die in an area no larger than one or two square miles and spends a predominant amount of his time in an even smaller area. He knows his homeland intimately and uses all of his senses to survive. He uses alternative feeding and bedding locations based on wind, seasonal food choices and personal preference.

Once a buck's antlers mature and he has removed the velvet, his habits change dramatically. He will move back into his brush- filled environment and as hunting pressure increases a smart old buck will slip into the thickest, most inaccessible brush patch he can find and will stay there

Mature bucks using cover to their advantage!

unless forced to move. During this time he becomes even more nocturnal, bedding well before daylight and only coming out to feed at or after dusk.

A mature, blacktail buck is a crafty, cautious animal and is a master of evasion. He's a lover of dense brush, secret pockets and alternative escape routes. He's seldom a runner, choosing rather to "wait it out". If he feels that he's not been discovered he will allow a hunter to walk within a few feet of his hideout without moving.

But if he thinks that he's been discovered, he will explode in a short brush breaking burst of speed. A fleeting glimpse of buckskin and branches is all a hunter may see as the buck of his or her dreams disappears into the all too available cover. More often than not though, a buck will let you pass or will quietly sneak out well ahead of your approach. When he rapidly flees, it's only for a short distance. Two or three thumps, then silence, as he quickly reverts to his quiet cautious behavior. A doe or yearling buck may run blindly through the woods for several hundred yards but not a wise old buck. He knows his escape routes and he uses them as strategically as possible.

Here is what some writers who have hunted all species of deer and big game have to say about the blacktail deer: Erwin Bauer in his book, *Deer In Their World* says, "No other horned or antlered species is as difficult to observe long enough to judge on the hoof as the whitetail. The only one as tough or tougher would be the blacktail...My own experience is that they (blacktails) are the hardest to find and photograph." Norm Nelson in the *American Hunter* says, "I've taken Northern Whitetails, Rocky Mountain Mule Deer and Columbia Blacktails. Without hesitation, I vote the blacktail as the toughest to hunt." Dwight Schuh says in the 1986 issue of Outdoor Life's *Deer Hunters Yearbook* "Blacktails offer a hunting challenge matched by few deer, and the hunter who can take big blacktails regularly has a lot of hunting savvy, I've had some experiences with whitetails, often touted as America's smartest deer, and I'd bet on the average blacktail's craftiness in contest with the average whitetail." Jim Zumbo in the March 1990 issue of the *American Hunter* has this to say, "When it comes to deer, blacktails just might be the ultimate challenge. The more I hunt them, the more I believe it. If you're a whitetail or trophy mule deer hunter and scoff at this statement, challenge a buck in his timbered bailiwick, one on one. Once you do, I'll wager you won't scoff anymore."

A very large, mature blacktail buck with good food and genetics, has antlers which measure 16 to 20 inches across and sport three to four points to a side. Wider antlered bucks exist but are rare. He may have eye guards, but the lack of eye guards, even on mature bucks, is common. His antler shape is similar to a mule deer, only smaller. The main beams generally start to curve inward at or about the ears and the tines continue to curve inward rather than straight up or out at the top like a mule deer. Many times a set of antlers which has an outside spread of 16" to 20" inches will have an inside tip to tip spread of only six or eight inches. The largest scoring buck which I have taken, scored 145 1/8 Boone and Crockett points, yet he had a tip to tip spread of under six inches.

It's common for three point bucks to have antlers which look very similar to a whitetail, with all of the points branching off the main beams. Non-typical antlers are very rare though there are enough of them that Pope and Young now has a non-typical classification and hopefully Boone and Crockett will eventually see the light and will also include a non-typical classification.

I'm not sure what the official weight of the largest blacktail deer is, but the largest buck which I have heard about

Photo credit: Boyd Iverson

My largest scoring buck. Great mass, very symmetrical, with long points, but the tip to tip spread is under 6 inches. B & C score: 145-1/8

weighed between 220 and 250 lbs., live weight. The biggest buck I have ever shot weighed in at 200 lbs., though I have shot several bucks which weighed in the 175 to 180 lb. range. The average, mature blacktail buck, from Oregon, weighs between 120 and 140 lbs. The body weight of black-tails in Washington tends to be greater than in Oregon and California.

Compared to the height, weight and antler spread of a large mule deer, the blacktail deer is a small animal. But judged on the difficulty of the hunt, involving the typical blacktail terrain and the intelligence of the animal hunted, a large blacktail buck is a real trophy. I would rate a record class blacktail as one of the most difficult hunting accomplishments in the United States, especially if you hunt them in the brush-filled habitat of Western Oregon and parts of Washington and British Columbia. The more open areas of

Southern Oregon and Northern California can sometimes be easier and allow some spot and stalk hunting opportunities similar to open country mule deer hunting.

Except in those areas mentioned above in Southern Oregon and Northern California, if you expect to hunt blacktails like you do mule deer, in the wide open spaces with high powered optics, you'll generally be disappointed. Also, if you're used to seeing large numbers of deer everyday be prepared for a let down. *Hunting blacktails relies more on analyzing and interpreting sign than the actual sighting of animals. Blacktail hunting is usually based on "faith", not sight.* The number of deer per sq. mile is statistically high in good blacktail country (it can be as high as 80 to 150 deer per sq. mile) but because of vision blocking and sheltering vegetation, the number of deer sighted per square mile is very low.

My own personal interaction with the blacktail has been long lasting, if not always successful. It started in my early

Photo credit: Boyd Iverson

Author checking tracks.

years, when I read my first deer hunting article and I felt that my greatest accomplishment in life would be to simply kill a blacktail buck, any blacktail buck! My fascination continued, with the reading and rereading of countless hunting magazines, which simply whetted, but did not curb, my enthusiasm.

While my friends took their annual trip with their dads to Eastern Oregon to hunt mule deer, I tromped up, down, over and through the brush covered canopy of Western Oregon.

Finally at the age of 12 I had "come of age" and could actually carry a rifle and enter the woods in pursuit of a real live deer. That first year I was fortunate enough to shoot a buck (though it was definitely more by accident than by skill) and my fascination has continued ever since.

I can still vividly recall the entire episode in my mind. I was walking up an old skid road after a heavy rain and was doing nothing particularly right. Fortunately for me, neither was the buck I shot. He had been spooked by another hunter and came racing over the top of the hill from the opposite direction. We saw each other at about the same instant and he put on the brakes as I raised my gun, but because of the slick dirt and his rate of travel he slid for a few feet before being able to change directions. This allowed me just enough time to put the peep site behind his shoulder and fire. The shot was well placed, though a little far back and the buck would have quickly laid down and died except for the fact that every time he laid down, there I was running behind him. So up he'd jump and stagger a few more yards before collapsing again. Finally my continued pursuit exhausted him and he gave up. So much for my first professional, cool, calm hunting excursion.

I have hunted blacktail deer for 38 years now and I have had the excitement of taking several large bucks, but the intensity of the experience has not diminished. My heart beats so loudly when I see a large buck, I'm afraid the deer will hear it. The blood rushes to my head so fast that, at times, I develop headaches and become weak-kneed and shaky and in a stalking situation I get so excited that I tend to move too fast and have to tell my mind to tell my body to slow down. I've even managed to pull the bolt completely out of my rifle while attempting to take a second shot!

Mine has not been the casual affair of hunting in the wide open spaces with a flat shooting rifle and high powered binoculars and spotting scopes, where shots are measured in hundreds of yards. Rather is has been, and still is, a close, intensely personal affair, involving sudden surprises, quick reflexes, and close encounters, where shots are measured in steps rather than hundreds of yards. This to me is what hunting blacktail bucks in the brush-covered habitat of Western Oregon is all about.

Recently I have learned to enjoy out of state, open country, spot and stalk, mule deer hunting but there's nothing like, one on one with a big blacktail buck.

The major emphasis of this book will be about the blacktail buck as I know him. I will talk about the strategies that I use and the styles of hunting which I practice, which I enjoy, and which have proved successful for me.

This is not to say that I know it all or that there are not other successful hunters or techniques. There are many productive hunting styles, and there are also various techniques for differing habitat, weather, and terrain. My personality enjoys the "one on one," close, quiet intimacy of still, and especially, stand hunting. These are the two hunting techniques I have worked at perfecting and which I will attempt to convey to you.

I have also included detailed chapters which should give you good guidelines for any big game hunting you may be involved in. These chapters, cover scouting, the use of scents and how to disguise human odor, general deer behavior patterns, animal identification techniques, optics, ballistics, rules for recovering wounded game and some interesting information regarding the various phases of the moon and how they *may* relate to the success of your hunt.

This book will not cover deer drives, deer calling or spot and stalk techniques, though these techniques can be, and are successful.

I honestly have had no great success with rattling in blacktails but I know of several archers who have been very successful with this technique, so I will pass on the information I have obtained from them and also information which I have read on antler rattling for whitetails. I believe that the whitetail is definitely a different animal, when it comes to habits, but the insight gained from these studies,

Photo credit: Boyd Iverson

First large buck I took from a pre-analyzed evening stand. In fact, this is the first buck I took after I decided to hunt only for larger bucks. B & C score: 108

Photo credit: Boyd Iverson

This is the only Boone and Crockett buck I've taken while still hunting. The antlers aren't heavy or wide, but there is great height and good length on all the points. He did lose about 7 points for non-symmetry. B & C Score: 131

I believe, will be applicable, because it relates to basic animal survival techniques common to all game animals.

As you continue to hunt you will develop the style of hunting you prefer. Continue to work at perfecting your techniques and you will be successful!

I hope that the information contained in my book will allow you to be a more successful hunter. But most of all I hope it will enable you to obtain more enjoyment out of your hunts, as you pursue this wonderful, elusive and frustrating animal called the blacktail deer.

One thing to remember though, is that it's easy to be "an expert" in a book; it's a lot harder in the woods. Just like you, I've hunted many days without seeing a buck. I have blown chances at big bucks and made stupid mistakes which have cost me deer, but I always try to learn from my mistakes and I keep trying. You can do the same. *Observation, analysis and persistence are the key attributes of all successful hunters.*

The more time you spend in the woods analyzing the deers' habits, studying a particular hunting location or just getting accustomed to the ebb and flow of nature, the more successful you will become.

It's very important to remember that even mature bucks are not "super human". Every year big bucks are taken by novice and experienced hunters and one of these years one will be taken by you if you're willing to "pay your dues."

THERE IS TYPICALLY NO "QUICK FIX" FOR TAKING TROPHY BLACKTAILS, NO MAGIC OR INSTANT POTIONS! TIME SPENT IN THE WOODS, PLUS OBSERVATION AND ANALYSIS, EQUALS ULTIMATE SUCCESS! LEAVE OUT ANY PART OF THIS EQUATION AND YOUR SUCCESS WILL DIMINISH.

Big bucks are smart, but they have weaknesses, and we need to learn how to use these weaknesses to our advantage, while at the same time minimizing our own shortcomings. *A deer acts and reacts by a combination of instinct and intellect.* We need to learn to use our intellect to outwit their instincts, while at the same time improving our own neglected senses.

I spent seven years compiling the material included in my first book and I've spent the last two years re-analyzing and adding to this information. At this point I can honestly say, that this book is as good as I can make it, and outside of actually living it like I've lived it, you now know what I know, or at least the portion of my knowledge which can be conveyed in words and placed on paper. So now it's up to you to apply this information and that's where the satisfaction and feeling of accomplishment come in!

Good Hunting!!

Chapter 2

To Be or Not to Be

Hunter Ethics

That is the question? Ethics and the Hunter. What's acceptable and what's not? What's right and what's wrong? What's more important; what's on the wall or how you got what's on the wall, the hunt or the hunted?

These are all questions which we need to ask ourselves to give us a guide for correct actions in the field. In recent years some "famous" hunters have become "infamous" because of actions they have taken to regain or retain their notoriety. The pressure to perform, in a very uncertain

33

sport can cause people with the desire to take large trophy animals, or the desire for fame or money, to choose unethical and unsportsmanlike behavior.

Ours is one of the only, if not the only sport, where we are not only the participant but also the spectators, the referee, the judge and the jury! This emphasis places a high burden of sportsmen and sportswomen like behavior on our part, as well as leaving us vulnerable and open to temptation when questionable situations arise in our pursuit of game. This is not to say that even ethical hunters will never make a mistake or use bad judgement, but there's a big difference between a single occurrence of bad judgement and a common practice of continual planned purposeful violations. Let's not be too quick to crucify somebody for making a mistake, but intentional game violators should be handed the maximum penalty.

We owe it to our sport to be the best that we can be and to police our ranks to help insure that hunting has a future.

Oregon Hunters Association, with Leupold and Stevens Inc. as the main sponsor, has set up a program call the T.I.P., or Turn in a Poacher Program. This program sets up a reward system for turning in game violators and is set up on an anonymous basis so that you do not have to give your name and information if you don't want to. This program has been responsible for numerous convictions and we should all know and use this 1-800 number, not because there's a reward at stake, but because the image of "hunters" is at stake. Poachers and game violators are not hunters, but they are the ones who get the publicity and the general public looks at them as if they portray what hunting is about.

Several years back I had one of my bucks taken and the guy went all over the small town where he lived bragging about the big buck he shot. He had his picture taken and he even took the head to a taxidermist to have it mounted.

What satisfaction there was for this individual, to look up at a buck on his wall which he had stolen from someone else is beyond my understanding. Luckily for me a neighbor who had read about my stolen buck in a Register Guard article called me and showed me a picture she had taken of the guy with my buck, and the police were able to stop his game.

I propose that the means by which we take game animals, the special conditions or circumstances surrounding the taking of the animal, the physical challenges involved in the taking of the game, the natural beauty or remoteness of the area hunted, the perfection of a well placed shot, the success of a correctly executed stalk on an unsuspecting quarry, the science of correct stand placement or posting on a possible escape route, or just the "magic of the moment" are what make "The Hunt."

Sure, we all like to take "trophy animals", but if our only judgement of a trophy is based on some books created measurement system then we have missed the point!

We as Americans seem to need a measurement of comparison and these scoring systems give us the means by which to do this, and I, as much as anyone, appreciate and am awed and amazed by a set of massive antlers, but I know personally, that I am more interested in the story behind the animal, to see how and under what circumstances the trophy was taken. That to me is the "true measurement" of a hunter or a hunters trophy.

Beyond merely the legal requirements we all need to decide our own personal standards. I have personally set up some standards which I try to live by. I have no serious physical impairments which necessitate that I hunt on or close to roads and personally have no desire to look for, or

Photo credit: Boyd Iverson

Large 4 x 4 which I shot, which was stolen by unethical "hunters". His B & C score was affected because he did not have deep forks and lacked one eyeguard. B & C score: 117

shoot, game from a vehicle. If I do happen to see a game animal from a vehicle and it continues on into the woods I will possibly pursue it under fair chase situations, but I make no attempt to look for game and I keep my rifle locked securely inside my rifle case while traveling in my hunting area.

But as previously stated, my choice of hunting is one on one, and as far away from roads, vehicles and people as I can get. I have nothing against shooting deer at what I consider long distances (100 to 200 yards) given the proper equipment, practice and correct conditions, but I prefer the up close and personal encounters.

To me that is what blacktail hunting is all about. But we all have our personal preferences and style, therefore we all need to decide what "The Hunt" means to us and then abide by those standards.

I have friends who hunt only with bows. I have friends who hunt only with traditional bows or muzzle loaders. I have friends who are excellent riflemen and enjoy and are good at long range hunting. There is nothing innately right or wrong with any of these styles of hunting.

What *is* important is, that each of these individuals has determined what "The Hunt" means to them and they will not compromise their ideals just to "hang an animal on the wall". I know a very good bow hunter, named Pete Garner, who wounded a large buck and was not able to recover it that day. He went back to camp that evening and was going to search for the buck the following day. When he got up the next morning it had snowed over a foot during the night and he was unable to even get within five miles of where he had shot the deer. He tried again the next day and the same story. At this point it had snowed approximately 3 feet and he knew that his deer would be completely covered and any further search at this point would be fruitless. His only choice was to come back in spring, as soon as the snow melted from the area.

He didn't even consider continuing his hunt, for him the season was over. This archer had a strong sense of right and wrong and his morals controlled his actions.

He came back a few months later when things warmed up a little to look for ravens or coyotes, but no success. One thing was on his mind during this entire time, finding *his* buck. Finally he came back the next spring after the snow melted and found his trophy. The animal had not traveled far from where he had found the last sign, but as expected the snow had totally covered the animal.

This is the kind of dedication and determination that we all need as hunters and sportsmen and sportswomen.

Determination pays off! Here are two photos of Pete Garner's mule deer. One photo of him and his mounted buck and one where he found the antlers.

This is Pete's story in his own words.

I was bow hunting at the 4,000 foot elevation November 17th. 1996 and saw a very large buck which I then stalked and got a shot at.

After the shot I went to where he was standing and found my arrow. It was completely covered with blood. After picking up my arrow I went back to my truck and waited with my friend Rich Reeves, for one hour. At 12:00 PM we started tracking. After going 200 yards I found a small piece of intestine that had hooked on a knot as the buck jumped over a log. Suspecting a gut shot I told Rich that we should wait some more.

After two more hours we picked up the trail again. The buck was traveling in the bottom of a draw and he is jumping, covering 12 to 15 feet at a time.

After tracking him for more than a mile it was getting dark. I told Rich that I would take him home and that I would come back tomorrow and find my buck. I knew that the buck had to be dead and I felt that the way he was traveling down the draw, that he would probably stay in the draw until he died.

I came back the following morning and had to cross a 4,500 foot high mountain pass. At this point, it was snowing so hard that I had to put chains on my four wheel drive pickup to get over the pass.

I made it to the road which would take me to where I left the trail the previous day but I am now pushing over 2 feet of snow with my front bumper and I still have over five miles to go. It continued to snow and I had to turn back. I drove to a lower elevation and waited until after noon but the snow continued. I then decided to return home and try again the next day. By the next day it had quit snowing but it had snowed another foot or so and I was unable to even get as far as I did the day before.

I went back the following weekend and I was still unable to get to where I needed to be, with over two feet of snow covering everything. I realized that the buck was undoubtedly dead and buried under the snow. I decided that the only way I was going to retrieve this buck was to wait until the snow melted.

All winter long I watched the weather very closely. During Christmas and New Years, we had a warm rain come through which started melting the snow at the pass level. I made a trip over the mountain to check and found that there was still over three feet of snow covering everything.

On April 5th, 1997, I again went over the mountain to check. Although the snow was melting very fast, where the sun was hitting, I was still unable to get within walking distance. On April 9th I came back and was able to make it to the draw, to resume looking for *my* buck. Staying in the draw and only walking 20 minutes I came upon the remains of my buck. It appeared that the snow had been off him for a couple of weeks.

Pete Garner

Chapter 3

Just In Case
You Were Wondering

*Some Photos to Show
That, Yes These Techniques
Do Work on Mule Deer*

Since 1994 I have taken five nice mule deer. All of these bucks were taken on self guided, out of state hunts, and were taken using techniques described in my book. Certainly the terrain and habitat are totally different than what I'm used to and discuss in my book, but the principles still seem to apply. If you've never hunted mulies, give them a try.

Photo credit: Boyd Iverson

Photo credit: Boyd Iverson

Idaho 1995. This is an old timber buck with high, heavy antlers. He was tooth aged at 6 1/2 years old. The rear points on this buck are over 15 1/2 inches long. I worked up on this buck after he bedded in heavy brush, after his morning feeding period. He was shot at approximately 50 yards, after about an hour long stalk.

Wyoming 1997. This is my most interesting buck. He is actually a very symmetrical non-typical 6 x 6, with very little side to side variation. He was with two other large bucks and I took him on a late evening stand, as he was moving down through a finger of aspen and red brush, to feed. He was tooth aged at 8 years old.

Idaho 1994. This is my most symmetrical buck. He's almost a perfect 4 x 4, with eyeguards, and has the classic mule deer form. He was tooth aged at 8 years old. I spotted him at approximately a mile to a mile and a half away and I reached him after a two hour plus stalk, the last 200 to 300 yards of which were in my stocking feet. He was shot at approximately 80 yards.

Idaho 1996. This is a five year old 3 x 4, not counting eyeguards. He was bedded, with a group of other deer, on an open hillside and I crab crawled to within about 40 yards of them before shooting.

Photo credit: Doug Glass

Wyoming 1998. This is the youngest buck which I have taken. He was tooth aged at four years old. I would have guessed that he was much older. I was hunting on 5,000 acres and I shot this buck within 75 yards of where I shot my 6 x 6 the previous year. He was taken during the same late evening feeding situation. I think I've discovered a pattern here!

Just thought you might enjoy these photos. Several people have asked me if I thought that my techniques would work on other game animals. According to my research, they do!

Chapter 4

Beauty Is In the Eye of the Beholder

Definition of a Trophy

A trophy, as in beauty, is in the eye of the beholder and should be a personal goal, relative to every hunter, rather than a comparison. Create your own guidelines and don't worry about what criteria someone else has established.

If you decide to use antler size as your goal, remember that every area has varied antler size due to the genetics of the area, the mineral content of the soil, the nutrition content of the vegetation, and the age structure of the deer. Be sure to create a standard that is reasonable for the area you hunt.

I hunted an area once which had a lot of deer, but the large mature bucks had, at the most, small to average sized three point antlers. A four by four buck of any kind was a real rarity. It would have been silly for me to compare the deer I took here with even an average buck, from a good trophy producing area. It was easy to kill a buck but there was no future for large-antlered bucks (which was my goal), so I quit hunting there. It still continues to produce several bucks a year, but nothing of any size.

Your judgement standard may not even be involved with the size of the antlers, but rather with how interesting

Photo credit: Boyd Iverson

Though not making the record book this buck has beautiful form and is one of the prettiest mounts I have.

or symmetrical they are, the particular circumstances of the hunt, how the animal was taken or numerous other options.

The first buck I shot was definitely on the small side by antler comparisons, but it will always have a very special place in my "trophy" collection. It was my first buck and I couldn't have been more excited if it had a 30" spread.

You should establish your own set of hunting guidelines and go from there. Your standard may be simply to get out into the woods during hunting season and just see a deer or put meat on the table. If so, don't worry about it. Everyone should not be, nor are they meant to be "trophy hunters", as judged by antler size or configuration. *But whatever you decide, remember that the "trophy" is never more important than the means used to obtain it! Sportsmanship and the hunt should always come first.*

We should all work at respecting the animal we hunt. The thrill does not come in the killing of the animal, but rather in the challenge and excitement of trying to outwit an animal on its own terms and its own turf.

Trophy Hunting Takes Trigger Control:

To be a trophy hunter in the sense of antler size you have to learn how to exercise "trigger control". You can't shoot large bucks if you keep shooting small ones. How many times have we decided to shoot a small buck, only to have a much larger buck magically appear, now that our tag is filled.

In the brush-filled habitat in which I hunt, you generally do not see many bucks during a season's hunt and you may only see one or none which meet your expectations. In most cases you do not have the opportunity to study an animal prior to your encounter and the chances are good that if you decide to let him fade into the forest, you will never see him again.

When a respectable buck enters your sights, the natural tendency is for your trigger finger to curl inward. This sets off a reaction which causes you to punch out your tag, take out your skinning knife and prepare your drag rope.

To combat this instinctive response you should determine what you will settle for prior to the hunt and then decide not to compromise your decision, no matter what. Many years I have taken my deer on the last evening of the last day of the season and other years I have taken no deer at all. The first year I set up my personal standard, I passed up 26 bucks before I shot the buck I wanted.

Passing up that first buck was one of the hardest and best decisions I have ever made. But after letting the first buck go, it has become easier and easier. The next year I passed up a very nice three point at 7:30 A.M. of opening day. I didn't see another large buck (in fact I saw only two other legal deer the entire season) until the evening of the last day of the season. A large symmetrical three point buck came out of the woods about 40 yards away from my stand and fed on grass and scrubs for almost 15 minutes. I can't say that I wasn't tempted, but I was able to control my finger response.

This was one of the finest experiences I have had while deer hunting and I learned a great deal about a buck's reactions and responses while watching this buck. My discipline paid off though, when a few minutes later, a large four point buck emerged from the woods just before dark, trailing behind five does. A shot in the neck at 25 steps put his antlers on my wall. But even if I hadn't shot the four point, I felt good about letting the three point go and considered the season a success. This was the buck which I talked about in the previous chapter on hunter ethics, which was taken by other "hunters", when I left him overnight in the woods.

Many "trophy hunters" end the season with no deer at all, but they always have a lot of memories to put on the walls of their mind. *Certainly, the challenge and thrill in hunting should not be tied to the killing of an animal.*

I have learned much more about deer and received a lot more enjoyment by watching instead of shooting, than in all the years of my "see and shoot" mentality. By passing up lesser deer, you will learn valuable information about deer habits which will enrich your enjoyment of the out of doors and will ultimately make you a much more successful hunter.

Anyone can be a "trophy hunter" if he or she has the desire and willingness to put in the time and effort needed to accomplish their goal. There's always some luck in hunting, but it takes a lot of hard work and determination to be "lucky" consistently.

Trophy hunting takes a positive mental attitude. It only takes a second to fill your tag once the animal you want is sighted. How many times have we decided that there's nothing around, so we relax our senses, get up to stretch, carelessly step on a twig, or walk ahead without looking, only to have a deer we hadn't noticed go crashing off through the brush.

Only last season I missed an opportunity to take one of the largest blacktail bucks I've seen and it was totally my fault! I had researched an area the year before, where one or more large bucks had left their antler induced scars on several trees along a particular ridge. I had hunted this area the previous year with no success and had decided to "scout it out" this year to see if the buck or bucks were still there.

I worked through the area during mid-day to see what sign I could find. It was during the late muzzle loader season and I should have been more focused, but I was treating it more like an off-season scouting trip and was concentrating more on locating sign than looking for actual deer.

I had been "hunting?" for about an hour and was starting back down the ridge when I spotted several trees which were very heavily rubbed. But instead of looking around for the responsible party, I was concentrating on the rubs and saying to myself as I continued to walk, "yeah, the big boy's still around". I had taken only three or four steps when the "big boy", who was watching me at a distance of thirty or forty yards, broke into short a zig zagging run among the trees, that would have made any pro running back proud.

Needless to say I was caught off guard and was unable to get off a good shot. If I had been still hunting correctly and had stopped and used the binoculars hanging around my neck, to search the habitat around me, instead of focusing only on the past evidence of the buck's presence I would have more than a fleeting memory. The buck would be on my wall instead of in the woods. But Lord willing, there's always next year.

Our concentration and determination need to continue to the very end. The hunt's not over until a half hour after the sun slowly settles into the horizon on the last day of deer season and this half hour of evening shadows is some of the most productive time for big bucks, so don't give up!

Chapter 5

Life According to Boone and Crockett

What It Takes to Make "The Book"

This chapter is written for those longing to take a "Record Book Blacktail", and talks about what it takes to make the most widely known scoring systems, which are Boone and Crockett for rifle hunters and Pope and Young for archers. Both of these categories use the same scoring technique but use different minimum scores for entry. The Boone and Crockett minimum typical score is 130 for the all time record book and 125 for the awards book and Pope & Young's minimum is 90. Boone and Crockett has no non-typical classification or classification for bucks in velvet. Pope and Young does recognize non-typical animals and uses the same minimum score for bucks in velvet as they do for hard antlered bucks. The Pope and Young minimum score for a non typical blacktail is 110. In both of the above scoring systems each point is equal to an inch in antler length, inside width or circumference and points are deducted for lack of symmetry from side to side and abnormal points, over one inch in length.

It is my opinion that the Boone and Crockett scoring system is not the most equitable system for the animal or the hunter, since it is based on perfection and as we all know most animals, like most humans, are not perfect. *When you think about it, actually the most non-typical animal is a perfectly typical animal!!!*

How would you score on a scale of 1 to 10? But be that as it may, the Boone and Crockett, and Pope and Young Scoring Systems are the most firmly entrenched and the most widely accepted scoring systems and if you want to be a member, you have to play by their rules.

There are many non-typical or slightly abnormal animals which are true trophies which do not qualify for the Boone and Crockett Scoring System or are penalized because of their abnormalities and do not score as high as they could. True non-typical bucks are certainly rare, but I have seen enough of them that I believe that they deserve their own classification.

David Morris, author of "The Record Book for Oregon" has a non-typical section and has further set up three separate blacktail categories; one for Cascade Blacktails, one for Columbia Blacktails and one for Northwest or Coastal Blacktails.

The Cascade classification allows bucks to be entered that wouldn't be allowed under the Boone and Crockett

Photo credit: Jim Gipe

This is an exceptional, truly once in a lifetime, 6 x 7, buck taken by Jim Gipe in Washington in 1976. This buck does not get the recognition it deserves because Boone and Crockett has no non-typical classification. If scored, its non-typical score would be 172.

Photo credit: Boyd Iverson

Another once in a lifetime buck taken by Leon Carson in Oregon in 1994. Leon took this buck with a bow so this buck can be entered into the Pope & Young Record Book. Non-typical score is 158.

boundaries because of concerns about inter-breeding with mule deer. The separate Columbia and the Northwest or Coastal Blacktail classification allows the coastal bucks, which tend to have smaller more compact antlers, to compete with animals of similar habitat and genetics and not be judged against the antler size of the mid range blacktails which tend to be larger.

Two scoring systems which use gross scores and do not down grade for non-typical features are Safari Club International, and Buckmasters. Safari Club uses the same type of measuring system as Boone and Crockett and Pope and Young but does not deduct for non-symmetry. The minimum score required for entry into Safari Club is 105 for rifle and the minimum entry score for archery is 90. Bucks in velvet are measured the same as hard antlered bucks and then the score is adjusted downward by 2%.

Currently the Buckmasters scoring system is used only for whitetails. This scoring system uses a gross measurement but does not score the inside width. Since this system measures only the length and mass of antlers, not the vacant space between the two sides, Buckmasters feels that this is a better judge of the "trophy worth" of an animal.

Recently several outdoor writers have proposed using gross Boone and Crockett, and Pope and Young scores with no deductions for side to side inequalities, as a fairer way of comparing trophies, for those of us who enjoy doing such things. This would be my personal choice for the fairest scoring system, since it still gives credit for inside antler width but does not deduct for inequalities from side to side.

Please remember that this chapter of the book is being written solely about the various scoring systems as a basis of judging the "trophy" standards of an animal. If you haven't already, please read the previous chapter entitled "Beauty Is in the Eye of the Beholder" for a broader perspective of what a "trophy" is.

The widest antlered blacktail bucks are found in the more open terrain of northern California and southern Oregon. The more typical antlered blacktail bucks are found in the more brush-filled terrain of Western Washington and Western Oregon. If we remove some of the widest antlered bucks from our calculations, we are looking at an average inside spread for a large blacktail buck of around 17 inches.

The average large blacktail buck's ears are sixteen to eighteen inches across and are six to eight inches long, so

Photo credit: Boyd Iverson

This is my widest antlered buck. The tip to tip spread is 13 inches and inside spread is 17-1/2 inches, but because of his short rear forks, he did not make the record book. B & C score: 121

this gives you a good visual measuring device to judge a buck's antler width and height.

All of this is done to say what may already be all too obvious to most of you, that any time you see a buck with antlers wider or equal to the width of its ears, and which stick up noticeably above its ears, it's a trophy, whether it makes the record books or not!!

Of the 95 blacktail bucks scoring 135 points and above in the 23rd "Boone and Crockett Big Game Records Book", which covers deer submitted between 1995 and 1997, but not necessarily killed during these dates, 49 came from Northern California, 13 from Southern Oregon, 23 from Western Oregon, 10 from Washington and 1 from British Columbia.

Trinity, Mendicino, Humbolt and Tehamo were the leading counties in California, Jackson, Lane, Clackamus, Josephine and Linn were the leading counties in Oregon and Pierce and Whatcom were the leading counties in Washington.

Of the bucks scoring 140 points or above and taken from 1990 on, 24 were from Northern California, 2 from Southern Oregon, 6 from Western Oregon and 6 from Washington.

In judging antlers, mass is important and tip to tip width is impressive (though unscored), but what is of primary importance is length of main beam, inside spread, the length of all antler points and for Boone and Crockett, and Pope and Young scoring systems, side to side symmetry. My largest buck, which scored 145 1/8 points, only had about three points deducted for lack of symmetry and had a tip to tip spread of under six inches.

Typically a mature four by four blacktail buck will be weak (short tine length) in either the front or rear forks and will lack eye guards. Many times a very large, old buck will develop a non-typical fifth point between the normal forks, on one side only, which will cost it several points in the Boone and Crockett and Pope and Young scoring systems.

These two bucks pretty much have it all; good mass, long deep forks and side to side symmetry. B & C scores are 138-7/8 and 145-1/8 and the side to side deduction for lack of symmetry is only 2-5/8 and 2-6/8 respectively.

Photo credit: Boyd Iverson

This is my heaviest bodied buck but he did not put a lot into antler development. He had a nice, wide, heavy, symmetrical set of 3 x 3 antlers with long tines. Notice how his antlers look a lot like a whitetails. His Boone and Crockett score was 107.

Photo credit: Boyd Iverson

This buck isn't wide and impressive but he has the longest eye-guards (4-1/2" and 3-1/2") of any buck I've taken. His net B & C score was 105 after 5 points of deductions for non-symmetry.

If you're looking for a "book buck", he would need to be at least a four by four, preferably with eye guards. This buck would be listed as a five by five in the Boone and Crockett, and Pope and Young Record books. It would need to have an outside spread which is equal to or wider than its ears and an antler height which is two and a half to three times the length of its ears. There would also need to be good main beam length, good depth on the forks and good length on all the forks. Also the points on either side would need to be evenly balanced. Obviously this is a lot to analyze before pulling the trigger and this is one of the reasons why I predominantly hunt from tree stands.

An average three point buck will score 70 to 80 points and an exceptional three by three with eye guards may score in the 120's. There are no three point bucks without eye guards, which make the 130 point minimum for the Boone and Crockett Record book, though I measured an exceptional three point buck with no eye guards, shot back in the 60's which scored an unbelievable 127 points. There are also no forkhorns which make the minimum Boone and Crockett Record Book, but I shot a very old and very large forkhorn with eyeguards, years ago, that scored a surprising 98 Boone and Crockett Points. (This buck, because of his eyeguards, would actually be listed as a 3 x 3 if he made the record books.)

An average four by four buck with eye guards will score between 90 to 100 points. A very nice four by four with no eye guards or a five by five blacktail buck (typically a four by four with eye guards) that does not have all of the needed antler length, is weak in the front or rear forks or lacks symmetry will score in the 115 to 125 range.

This information and the various photos throughout the book, which show the actual Boone and Crockett Score, are given to help those of you who want to hunt for a "book buck" and give you a standard of measurement by which to judge the bucks which you see. The scores on all of these bucks would be higher if scored by Safari Club's scoring system.

There are also many fine trophy animals which are not listed in the record books due to the fact that they live in that in-between zone of potential cross over areas between blacktails and mule deer. They score too high for the black-tail classification but do not score high enough to meet the minimum mule deer requirements. They are essentially a forgotten species, at least as far as the Boone and Crockett, and Pope and Young record books are concerned. To do justice to these animals and the hunters who pursue them there should be a separate classification set up for these animals so that they can get the recognition they deserve.

Boundaries for Mule and Blacktail Deer, As taken from the 1988 edition of Boone and Crocketts' *Records of North American Big Game.*

British Columbia—Starting at the Washington-British Columbia border, blacktail deer range runs west of the height of land between the Skagit and the Chilliwack Ranges, intersecting the Fraser River opposite the mouth of Ruby Creek, then west to and up Harrison Lake to and up Tipella Creek to the height of land in Garibaldi Park and northwesterly along this divide past Alta Lake, Mt. Dalgleish, and Mt. Waddington, thence north to Bella Coola. From Bella Coola, the boundary continues north to the head of Dean Channel, Gardner Canal, and Douglas Channel to the town of Anyox, then due west to the Alaska-British Columbia border, which is then followed south to open water. This boundary excludes the area west of the Klesilkwa River and the west side of the Lilloet River.

Washington—Beginning at the Washington-British Columbia border, the boundary line runs south along the west boundary of North Cascades National Park to the township line between R10E and R11E W.M., which is then followed directly south to its intersection with the north border of Mt. Rainier National Park, then along the north, west, and south park boundaries until it intersects with the township line between R9E and R10E W.M., which is then followed directly south to the Columbia River near Cook.

Oregon—Beginning at Multnomah Falls on the Columbia River, the boundary runs south along the western boundary of the National Forest to Tiller in Douglas County, then south along Highway 227 to Highway 62 at Trail, then south following Highway 62 to Medford, from which the boundary follows the township line between R1W and R2W E. W.M. to the California border.

California—Beginning in Siskiyou County at the Oregon-California border, the boundary lies between townships R8W and R9W M.D.M., extending south to and along the Klamath River to Hamburg, then south along the road to Scott Bar, continuing south and then east on the unimproved road from Scott Bar to its intersection with the paved road to Mugginsville, then south through Mugginsville to State Highway 3, which is then followed to Douglas City in Trinity County, from which the line runs east on State Highway 299 to Interstate 5. The line follows Interstate 5 south to the area of Anderson, where the Sacramento River moves east of Interstate 5, following the Sacramento River until it joins with the San Joaquin River, which is followed to the south border of Stanislaus County. The line then runs west along this border to the west border of Santa Clara County. The east and south borders of

Santa Clara County are then followed to the south border of Santa Cruz County, which is then followed to the edge of Monterey Bay.

Chapter 6

Picture Perfect

*How to Create Good Taxidermy
and Take Good Photos*

Don't blame your taxidermist if your trophy of a life-time looks like a dead stuffed deer!! He can only work with what you supply him, though I have seen taxidermists create some very good looking mounts from some terribly neglected game animals.

Good taxidermists can sew up careless knife cuts, close up gaping holes caused by high powered rifles, reattach ears, touch up antlers and do any number of amazing tricks, but why should we make their jobs more difficult? With a little bit of fore-thought and caution you can benefit yourself and your taxidermist.

Photo credit: Boyd Iverson

This sitka blacktail had to have its ear replaced after it was eaten by a martin. Bet you can't tell which one!

I have found that many animals are not mounted because of lack of knowledge, both of the process by which to preserve a trophy and by misconceptions about the cost and the process of mounting a trophy.

I have heard comments such as; "$350 for a full shoulder mount, I thought it cost $500", "well, after I cut its throat the cape was ruined", "after the deer was down I ran up to it and put a bullet in its skull to finish it off", "I got the deer during the first day of the hunt and by the time I got the animal home the hide was ruined", and finally, "my grandfather helped me skin the animal and while I was at the store buying film he cut the head off right below the neck".

All or these mistakes could have been easily remedied if the people had followed some simple advice and knew some general information about mounting a trophy. As my grandmother used to say, "An ounce of prevention is worth a pound of cure."

NO NEED TO BLEED: With the use of today's high powered rifles and razor sharp broadheads, there is no need nor benefit in cutting a deer's neck to let it bleed. Also, shooting a deer in the head or neck at close range with a high-powered rifle is a good way to damage the deer as well as yourself!

THE RIGHT STUFF: Carry a small camera and tape measure. If possible take photos of your trophy from all angles. Take measurements of the length of the nose from the tip of the nose to the eye, the width of the nose, and measurements of the circumference of the neck just below where the neck meets the head and the circumference and thickness of the chest.

THINK BEFORE YOU CLEAN: If you want a full head and chest mount, do not cut open the body cavity any further than the sternum (the heavy bone that the ribs connect to), keep blood and dirt off the cape and do not drag the animal along the ground with the hide on.

A shoulder mount needs the hide well past the shoulder and if you drag the animal you will damage and or remove hair from this area. Rubbed off and broken hair is one thing that the taxidermist cannot replace. I know because the first Boone and Crockett Buck I killed, I dragged for over a mile and managed to permanently mar an other wise perfectly good cape.

PROPER CAPING TECHNIQUES: If you decide to remove the hide yourself, cut all the way around the deer in a circular motion six to eight inches behind the deer's shoulder or in line with where you stopped your cleaning-out process at the sternum. Then make a cut up the back of the neck to just behind the antlers. Next, cut the hide at the knee joints on both of the front legs all the way around and then remove both legs below the knee. Finally, skin out the leg completely in a tube without cutting the leg further or cut down the back side of the leg where the dark hair meets the white, all the way up to where the leg meets the shoulder. Once this is done, complete the skinning job up to and around the neck, just below the ears, being careful not to cut through the skin. Remove as much of the wind pipe as possible and cut off the deer's neck right below the head.

If you can't get to a taxidermist within a day, put non-iodized salt on the exposed portions of the hide and in the eyes, ears, and nose openings and store the cape in the driest, coolest place available or if possible put the hide and head in a freezer. If you're going to be out for several days keep the hide opened up and continue to add salt to the cape on a daily basis. I use five to 10 pounds of salt per cape.

I don't recommend fully caping out the head yourself unless you have too. The taxidermist is a lot better at it than we are.

If you're planning on hunting during the time when a deer's antlers are still covered with velvet be sure and take along a small bottle of formaldehyde, a couple of hypodermic needles, at least one pair of disposable plastic gloves and some protective eye glasses. Inject this solution into all velvet covered areas—starting at the tips of all the antlers and working down until all the blood is out of the veins and they run clear at the base of each antler—being careful not to get any of the liquid on your skin or in your eyes. FORMALDEHYDE IS AN EXTREMELY HARSH CHEMICAL AND WILL BURN THE SKIN AND CAN SEVERELY BURN YOUR EYES. ALSO BE CAREFUL NOT TO BREATH THE FUMES! The formaldehyde will preserve the velvet and keep it from spoiling.

Note: Remove the cape from the skull, before injecting the formaldehyde, as the formaldehyde will ruin the cape if any gets on it.

If you decide to strip the velvet from the antlers, you can then submerge the antlers in cold water and the blood will come out, leaving the antlers almost bone white. These antlers can later be stained by your taxidermist to a natural brown color.

If you can't afford a full mount at the time you take your trophy you can simply have the head portion of the hide tanned (cost $50 to $75) and have the deer mounted with the antlers later. But remember that a full head and shoulder mount costs only about $350 and can usually be paid for in installments.

If you've already taken an animal which you would like to mount but did not save the cape, or it was somehow ruined, all is not lost. You can still take the antlers to the taxidermist and he can match the antlers with capes he has in stock and make an excellent looking mount for you.

Since we are talking about taxidermists, I would like to say that all taxidermists are not created equal. As in any profession there are good ones, average ones and excellent ones. Check the mounted animals which they have in their shop, for realism and life-likeness. *A good taxidermist will make a dead animal look alive! If all the animals you are looking at, look dead, keep looking!!*

Be sure and ask the taxidermist if they fully tan their capes before mounting rather than a pickle or rub on tanning process. A tanned cape makes for a better looking and longer lasting mount. Once you have chosen the taxidermist, look at his various mounts to determine which style or pose will best fit the room you plan to place your trophy in.

For many of us mounting a game animal will be a once in a lifetime occurrence, for others it may be a yearly hap-

Comparison of bad and good taxidermy.
Top: This is the mount of my stolen buck which was confiscated by the police. Bottom: Photo of the same buck mounted by a professional taxidermist.

Photo credit: Boyd Iverson

Though this buck doesn't have large antlers, he is still a very beautiful trophy. He's also the oldest buck I have taken since I started tooth aging all of my bucks. He was tooth aged at 9 years old.

pening. But however often it occurs, we owe it to the animals we hunt to preserve them in the best manner possible.

For those of you who don't have the money to have your animal professionally mounted, or those who want a permanent "Kodak Moment" in addition to the mount, think photograph!

Remember, that a good photo is forever and tells a story in itself, so let's try to tell good stories by our photos. A good, properly planned photo is a great memory maker.

If you follow a few fairly simple procedures you can create some good to great photographs. Let's try to end the photos of a buck with its tongue hanging out of its mouth or covered in blood, the buck hanging from the garage ceiling, the bloody buck laying in the back of the pickup or tied to a four wheeler, the photo of an obviously dismembered buck head or any of the other photos which do not give proper respect to the game we pursue and the sport we enjoy.

SOME RULES TO FOLLOW:

1. Use a good, compact, 35 millimeter camera, preferably with a telephoto zoom lens, self timer, and a built-in flash with red eye reduction capabilities. If possible carry a small tripod. There are several companies which make very small light weight tripods. For the best photos always carry the camera and a couple of rolls of film into the field with you. There are several water proof compact cameras on the market. I use a Pentax 105WR. I also place my camera inside a zip lock baggie. If you can't afford a real camera at least carry one of the small, throw away, cameras on the market. They will at least give you some good memories.

2. Use 400 speed film, since most times animals are taken in less than ideal light situations.

3. ALWAYS CLEAN UP ALL BLOOD, COVER OR CONCEAL ANY BULLET OR ARROW HOLES AND MAKE SURE THAT THE DEER'S TONGUE IS INSIDE ITS MOUTH AND ITS MOUTH IS NOT HANGING OPEN.

4. You can liven up a photo by putting water on the deer's nose and eyes to make them glisten.

5. Compose your photo to make sure that there are no distracting elements in the picture. Clear obscuring vegetation, branches or shrubs that look like they are part of the deer or hunter, remove anything that takes your eye away from the animal either in the foreground or the background.

6. Analyze how the antlers look in the photo and make sure that all of the points are easily visible.

7. If possible take a picture with you and the animal.

8. If you do a self-posed photo with a timer or have a hunter in the photo, be careful of hats which can hide or cast a shadow on the hunter's face. Most of todays small compact cameras come with built in flashes and I would

suggest using them even during day light hours to help eliminate shadows.

9. When you're composing the photo, place the hunter off to one side and slightly behind the deer and make sure that his hands do not obscure the antlers. Be sure to again recheck to make sure that the antlers are at the correct angle and all of the points are clearly visible.

10. Take pictures from a variety of angles (standing, kneeling, prone)and a variety of perspectives. FILM IS CHEAP!!! TAKE LOTS OF PHOTOS!! I usually take 30 or 40 photos and out of these I hope to get two or three that look just the way I want.

11. Don't shoot into direct sunlight and watch for shadows when shooting with the sun behind you. As mentioned above, it's a good idea to use the automatic flash for fill in, even during the day.

12. Try to avoid the photos with the hunter behind the buck with his arms fully out stretched holding the deer in front of him. This photo does make the deer look larger but it's also obvious what's being done. Let the animal stand on its own merits.

If you haven't followed these rules, or haven't been able to make the animal look presentable, then you still have one more option. With modern computer technology photos can be touched up and changed as needed, so if you have a favorite animal with a less than favorite composition take it to a professional photo shop and see what they can do.

Recently I had a photo taken of me with a nice mule deer I took in Wyoming in 1998. When we composed the photo we thought that a natural shadow would hide the bullet hole. Unfortunately we were wrong. So I took the negative to a photo shop and they "digitally remastered" the photo, made the bullet hole disappear and made a new negative. The new photo looks great!!

You can see this photo in the chapter entitled "Just in Case You Were Wondering" and I bet you won't be able to tell where the touch up work was done.

Also under the section of the book entitled "Readers Photos", you can see examples of a lot of good and some very good photos. Take a look and see what you like and try to duplicate it in your personal photos.

I hope that the information in this chapter will help you make the best out of your trophy animals and memories.

Chapter 7

Scouting for Success

Initial Overview, Use of Maps and Aerial Photos, Trail Analysis, Sound and Scent Containment, Game Spotting Techniques and more

Most of us would never consider taking a trip to some new town or city without first looking at a map but it's always surprising to me how many people go out on opening day of deer season without any prior analysis of their hunting area and march boldly into the woods expecting success. They usually get in a lot of hiking, but contrary to popular opinion, hiking isn't hunting!! Consistently successful hunting needs to have a predetermined plan. The first and most important item to complete before you begin any season, is to scout your prospective location so you know what to expect *before* you enter the woods.

Scouting is the art of analyzing a particular geographic area (the more specific the better), locating potential feeding and bedding locations and discovering the various interrelationships of the trails traveling to, through, and out of these two locations. You want to discover the travel patterns and the time of activity on these trails in relation to the time and use of these feeding and bedding locations. You're looking for a general over-view of the activity patterns.

The forest is in a constant, though sometimes gradual state of change. If you continue to hunt in the same location you will discover that these patterns change depending on the time of the year, food supply, wind and weather conditions and breeding activity. They will also change as the habitat grows up and matures, or is logged or altered by natural forces.

The first requirement I look for is an area which has a history of large bucks. Genetics, soil types, and food sources are the key elements which promote larger antler growth and they work together to produce trophy-sized bucks.

The area you settle on may be a large generalized location covering several thousand acres or a very small centralized area such as a particular canyon or ridge. Typically the more centralized and focused you become the more successful you'll be, as long as you've chosen a productive area in the first place. I find that if I attempt to learn too large an area and do not centralize I become less successful.

If you study an area long enough you will find that in any given habitat there are specific locations which hold more deer and areas which historically hold the larger bucks.

It's best to locate an "inaccessible area" to keep other human intrusion to a minimum. Constant human activity will cause the larger bucks to interrupt their normal patterns and become more secretive and nocturnal. When I talk about "inaccessible", I'm referring to an area which is overlooked by other hunters because of its distance from major road systems, difficult or questionable access due to land ownership or because it is "too steep, rough or brush-filled". In my opinion such an area should be a minimum of one to two miles from traveled roadways. The exception to this would be a very rugged or brush-filled habitat which is ignored not because of its distance from roads but because of how difficult it is to get to.

People sometimes tell me no such areas exist where they hunt, and that there are roads everywhere. But I guarantee you that these areas do exist and if you'll spend the time and get a current BLM map, topo map, or better yet, an aerial photograph, you can and will locate areas other hunters ignore.

With a current aerial map you will be able to get a good bird's eye view of the interrelationship of all the various roads, clear cuts and points of interest. This will tell you a lot about potential hunting spots and why, where, and how deer travel from one location to another.

The average hunter will not take the time to do the research you are willing to do, but if you put in the effort you will see and shoot a lot more game and have a better chance of obtaining the trophy you desire. There isn't any canyon or brush patch I wouldn't go into if I believed that there were big bucks hiding there!

I like to locate mixed terrain and habitat and I want the area to supply the deer with a variety of food, bedding and cover options.

Some examples would be: the edges of 2 to 5 year old clear cuts (usually used right at or after dark) with heavier timber or other appropriate security cover nearby and away from traveled roads; small openings in older clear cuts, say eight years or older, where grasses and scrubs have grown instead of trees (used during early morning mid-day if protected enough, and late in the evening or after dark); mature forests where you find a mixture of deciduous and coniferous trees with small protected grassy or brush covered openings, any benches (i.e., small level areas in otherwise steep terrain) where better soil, water, nutrients, and additional sunlight have caused better plant growth, natural or man-made openings in the forest which allow in more sunlight than surrounding areas; the edges of moist locations or drainages which produce a variety of nutritious plants; and the lower edges of older clear cuts, when these areas are out of the eyesight of other hunters or not easily driven to.

These older clear cuts are used in early morning and just before dusk and are especially good choices to check the first few days of early archery season and the final few

Photo credit: Boyd Iverson

The habitat shown in the background of this photo is perfect, at least in the areas I hunt.

days of the rifle season. Also check these locations during the later archery or muzzle loader seasons, when the rut is on, because does will gravitate to these locations and the bucks will follow the does.

Look for small protected openings with good surrounding cover or larger openings if there is sufficient vegetation to provide a sense of security for any mature buck who decides to feed there. The proverbial apple tree in the center of a clearing or a large wide open clearing is "not" a good bet. A big buck will feel too exposed to enter such an area during daylight hours. *Big bucks need cover, either vegetative cover or the cover of darkness.* They will feed in open exposed areas, but usually only after dark.

Once you've located such a spot the work and the fun begins as you attempt to put all of the pieces of the deer behavior puzzle together.

Remember that "feeding locations" are numerous and sometimes indistinct, since blacktails are browsers and their food sources are varied and not concentrated in any one location. I like to locate mixed terrain and habitat and I want the area to supply the deer with a variety of food, bedding and cover options.

Heavy old growth timber gives good security cover, is cooler in summer and warmer in winter, and can be an effective area for still hunting during nasty weather but it does not provide much food. It is an area that deer may bed in and pass through to get from one area to another, but deer do not spend time feeding here unless there is a very wet fall which produces a heavy crop of mushrooms. Even then it's not a centralized feeding location, but is rather a "grab as you go" proposition as deer move through on their way to other destinations.

Except in very dry areas, water sources are not a controlling factor in blacktail behavior and I do not hunt in dry habitat.

Look for secluded hillsides above feeding locations, covered with a combination of firs, ferns and a liberal scattering of deciduous trees such as maples, alders, or ash. Maples, alders and ash trees will be found along moist draws, water ways and benches. This type of habitat makes ideal blacktail hunting grounds. The types of vegetation will vary from area to area but the general principals of analysis apply in all situations.

In the spring deer will seek out those foods highest in nutrients. The south and west facing slopes will receive most of the activity in early spring and summer because these locations receive the first sunlight and greatest plant growth. But these areas will get burned out by late August and the deer turn to the damper, color, shaded east and north facing locations for their food sources or they will move into the moist draws and gullies on south and west facing slopes.

After August or the first week of September, when the bucks have satisfied their high protein requirements needed for antler development, the amount of deer sign both in the form of deer sightings and in the form of deer activity diminishes until the bucks start thinking about the opposite sex around the first week in November.

Once bucks shed their velvet in late August or early September their personality and habits change abruptly. They become much more secretive, start to move away from their bachelor groups, create small sparring encounters to establish dominance, and move back into heavier more protective cover. They will remain in the same general area but will be less visible, or as some hunters claim, they will become "invisible."

As you are scouting make notes on which types of food are preferred at various times of the year and where the highest concentration of those foods are found. Take notes

Successful summer scouting. Photo by Curt Brace. This buck would score in the 140's to 160's.

Photo credit: Boyd Iverson

Two nice summer bucks as seen from a tree stand.

on bedding locations, old and new rubs, trail activity, dropped antler locations, specific deer sightings and how and why the animals enter and exit their various habitats. Make notes of any specific spots which stay green and lush long after other locations are brown and dry. In hot weather look for cool pockets and during cold weather locate habitat which is warmer. During wet and windy weather look for secluded pockets on the lee (opposite) side of the storm, which provide protection and shelter from rain and especially the wind.

I have never seen large bucks out in high wind situations. A deer's large ears are very sensitive and I believe that their hearing is adversely affected by high winds.

In your analysis, start first with a general overview and then culminate your research with some specific "hands on" application, i.e., get out and walk the area and begin to take notes on what you find.

In most, if not all, cases you are not trying to pattern an individual buck, but rather a specific area. You can discover general districts which hold trophy bucks by looking at the Boone and Crockett, and Pope and Young Record Books, or in Oregon take a look at the "The Record Book for Oregon" by David Morrison. Talk to game biologists, ranchers, farmers, loggers, delivery people (milk, paper) and other hunters. Do your own personal research and keep your eyes and ears open.

Always be careful not to step on or take advantage of another hunter's willingness to share information with you. If you intend to hunt in "his area" ask his permission first!

MAPS:

When you discover a promising area, then the real work begins. Now you need to find out land ownership to obtain permission to hunt if needed. This can be done using

These bucks will move apart as soon as they shed their velvet.

Metskers' maps, court house files or local title insurance companies. Purchase topography, BLM, or forest service maps and aerial photos.

For a point of reference, with a 7.5 minute topo map in 1:24,000 scale, 1" equals .38th of a mile and the contour lines are spaced at 10 feet intervals.

Now start getting specific. The topo map will show you the location of ridges, valleys, benches and the general lay of the land. Look for spots where the topo lines show cross-over saddles between two ridges, drainage ways and potential travel ways from ridge to ridge. In short, look for any information which will help you discover the logical pattern of movement.

In steep terrain, look especially for small areas on side hills or the ends of ridges where the topo lines become wider apart. This indicates a more level area and this particular habitat will attract deer. It does not need to be a large area; any level area will work, if it is situated correctly, even areas as small as 60 or 80 yards wide by 100 yards long. *Deer prefer to feed on and bed above or below these prime feeding locations.*

The aerial photos will show vegetation types, possible feeding or bedding locations, the overall interrelationships between the various openings in the woods, road access points or the lack of the same and possible logical travel patterns between potential feeding and bedding locations.

In your analysis, realize that *deer spend approximately 70% of their time bedded*, resting, digesting their food and sleeping, so the location of preferred bedding areas is very important. *All activity emanates from and leads back to these locations.*

You must also be aware that there are daytime bedding locations and evening bedding locations and the two are set up completely differently.

I could never figure this out as a kid. Here were all of these obvious deer beds, right out in the open, but I never could find a deer using them. Now I know, what might have been obvious to some, that these beds were only used at night.

The daytime beds are usually in thick cover and higher up on the hillsides. They are strategically placed so the animal has visibility below and wind protection from behind, and will provide one or more escape opportunities. Evening beds on the other hand are situated lower down and are out in the open to protect the deer from traveling predators who could easily sneak up on them in heavy cover, under the protection of darkness. The bedding locations that we as hunters are concerned with obviously would be the locations which are used during the day.

Look for the same type of information you tried to discover on the topo map. Locate vegetation changes from deciduous to evergreen (blacktails prefer to feed in fringe areas). Find small openings which could be potential feeding spots and fingers of timber or brush which provide cover between these feeding and bedding locations. Look for overgrown skid roads, swales, saddles, and other protected travel ways from feeding to bedding locations in the morning and bedding to feeding locations in the mid-day or the evening.

The mid-day feeding patterns will be short forays from their bedding locations and they generally will stay within, or very close to, good security cover.

Next try to find a high vantage point from which to analyze the vegetation types, drainage ways, ridges and potential travel corridors. A good pair of high quality optics (10 plus power binoculars, 20 plus power spotting scope) is a great advantage for this type of work. If you cannot find a high vantage point, you can make your own by using a light tree stand, and tree stand steps to climb above the height of the sight restraining brush or timber. Always carefully check your footing, the security of your tree stand attachment and use a safety belt while using any tree stand. *Serious tree stand injuries occur every year.*

It's a good idea to analyze the terrain in the springtime and after the trees have given up their leaves in the fall. You can get a much clearer picture of the terrain and potential travel patterns at this time of the year.

Now start physically inspecting what you have analyzed at a distance. You are looking for deer *sign*, not deer sightings. If you do see undisturbed game, so much the better, but you will have plenty of time to concentrate on spotting deer once the season begins. Makes notes of where you see the most activity. Determine where the major and minor trails are located, where they intersect, what their direction of travel is, what time of day the trails are used, bedding locations, escape trail locations, feeding spots, tree rubs and any other information you find which will benefit your hunting plans.

The best time to do specific scouting (in an area you are already familiar with), is during the hunting season. Whether it's after you get your deer, while passing up lesser bucks, or instead of going back to camp or car for your afternoon siesta. If you come upon an interesting trail, check it out! See where it goes or comes from and mark it on your map.

Scout immediately after the season too, as deer activity, trail, wind and weather patterns should be very similar to what they are during the season.

If, while scouting, you see one or more good bucks, you can be sure that there will be others. It usually takes five to eight years to produce a wide or heavy antlered rack and during this time a buck has had ample opportunity to spread his gene pool around the neighborhood.

But as I said in the introduction, most blacktail hunting is "by faith and not by sight", so don't worry if you don't see a lot of bucks. As long as the sign is there we can be sure that the deer will follow. I have never personally seen a particular trophy buck before the season and then subsequently taken him during the hunting season. I'm sure though, that I have seen the *sign* of several of the bucks which I have taken.

Trophy bucks are different. They're smart and super cautious. They have to be to have survived numerous hunting seasons and hundreds of hunters. Big bucks don't grow old by acting dumb. So if you want to consistently take large bucks, your intensive scouting should be done in the off-season and during times which are least disrupting.

Do not pollute the area you intend to hunt with your scent and human activity. Treat the off season scouting trips just like they were hunting trips except that in this case you do your off-season scouting in your chosen area during the time when the deer are least likely to be there. Follow the guidelines given in the chapter entitled Scents and Nonsense.

TRAVEL PATTERNS:

Obviously it is never this simple, but simply stated, deer are either traveling to bed or going to eat. As mentioned earlier, unless it is a very hot, dry, arid, area water sources are not prime factors in determining deer activity patterns. Deer can obtain most of their moisture requirements from their food.

You should attempt to locate the general feeding patterns and preferred bedding locations. Discover the trails that access these activities, during daylight hours, and determine what time of day they are used. Position yourself accordingly and you've got yourself a buck!

There are morning trails, early evening trails, nighttime trails and escape trails, Any of these trails will support varied activity, depending on the time of year (based on changes in food, weather, and the timing of the rut), time of day, reason for use and varying wind and weather conditions.

In your notebook keep notes on such things as wind direction, location and activity of deer seen, type and number of deer seen, time of day, direction of travel, condition of moon, temperature, weather, before and after the sightings, and any other information which you feel will help you solve the riddle. Play Sherlock Holmes and ask yourself questions about the assumptions you can make based on the information you have collected.

Since discovering the various travel patterns in an area can take a large amount of time, sometimes up to several years, and since we as humans can only be in one place at a time I have recently entered into the art of modern science and discovered a way to clone myself, by the use of trail timers. Yah, I know, hunting is getting to mechanized!

But the point is, by researching your area and placing trail timers at the specific locations you feel would be good potential stand sites, you can determine the exact time the trails are used and then you will know whether these locations are huntable.

And it's still not as simple as it sounds. There still are a lot of variables which affect the success of the location, even after determining the general times of travel. So it's not like you can set your timer, determine time of travel and go out and shoot a big buck every time you sit on your stand.

You still have to analyze wind direction, weather patterns, hunting pressure, time of year, period of the moon and similar considerations, and unless you use a trail timer with a camera you don't know if the deer which use the trail is the deer you want. But you at least have removed

Photo credit: Boyd Iverson

Author analyzing sign.

one variable in the equation and that is when the deer normally use the trail. Analyzing and discovering these other variables will determine the ultimate success of your hunting endeavors. At the back of the book, in the chapter entitled "Gizmos and Gadgets", I talk about the trail timer which I use and prefer, and why I prefer it over the other timers on the market.

TRAILS:

The first rule to remember is that deer always travel on trails; for ease of travel, for the sake of being quiet, and as a means of letting their noses inform them of what other animals

Photo credit: Chuck Bartlett

Trails are the animal world's scent saviors. Nothing passes without their notice!

have traveled ahead of them. *Trails are the gossip columns of the deer, or for that matter, the entire wildlife community.* Every animal which travels on the trail leaves a scent which can be detected by a deers' and other predators' keen sense of smell.

Remember that a deers' movements are not hap-hazard, they have a purpose and a pattern. It may not always be clear to us what that pattern is but it's clear to the deer!

Trails are a deers' highway. In typical habitat there are a few well-worn trails. These well worn trails are generally located along ridge tops (ridge top trails are generally night-time trails and thus do not benefit the hunter), near the deers' initial feeding location for their evening meal or in situations like saddles or swales where nature provides travel ways which provide natural screening. You will also find well worn trails along natural or man made funnels, where the topography, geography or man made constraints limit or centralize travel.

Otherwise, there are a multitude of indistinct feeder trails branching out in all directions and used as wind, weather and survival dictate. Although the major trails are the easiest to see (and we as humans seem to want to spend most of our time there), remember that the safest way for a large buck to travel is on the less conspicuous trails, "the path less traveled."

A bucks' typical travel pattern will be parallel to and down wind of major trails, except at night and sometimes during the rut. But even during the rut a buck will prefer to scent and sight check a major travel or feeding location rather than travel on it, at least until he has found the object of his affection.

If you can figure out the reason for the trails (food, escape, sex, bed) and the time of usage (general rule: downhill to eat in the evening and uphill to bed in the morning), in time, you can successfully learn how to hunt any given area or habitat.

TIME IS THE KEY ELEMENT IN THIS EQUATION! Rome wasn't built in a day and neither is the perfect hunting strategy! Be Patient!! Be Alert!! Be Observant!! Don't give up!!!

Take notes on wind directions and corresponding deer movement patterns. Continue to fine tune and update your notes and maps every year. *Figure out why the trails are used, when they are used, where they lead, and then structure your hunt accordingly.*

Look for logical travel points. Such areas could be brush choked ravines, finger ridges, swales, geographic funnels, benches, old overgrown skid roads, water ways, wooded areas extending into or across more open habitat and similar situations which are located between bedding and feeding areas. When you locate such trails, put them on your map and try to find out their relationship to the overall pattern of activity.

If you really want to discover how a deer travels and uses cover and the lay of the land to their advantage, spend several days just following existing trails, as they maneuver and move through a deer's environment. But don't spend your time on the most deeply cut trails, or the trails that follow along the tops of ridges or cut off the points of ridges, because these trails are normally used after dark and don't teach you anything about how a deer travels during daylight hours. Instead follow the more indistinct trails, which meander along side hills, cut through swales or low spots, work through fingers of cover and travel along the edges of cover.

While you're traveling on these trails analyze tracks to see what you can discover about the animals who are using the trails, but don't spend time on these trails for at least a month prior to hunting season. Again, the best time to do your research is just after the season ends or after you have filled your tag and you're wondering what you're going to do with your life.

All morning trails will follow the path of least resistance, will angle upwards from lower to higher ground and travel side hill along the ridges. They will cross over ridges at low spots or saddles in order to travel with the wind in their faces or crosswise to the wind, and provide visibility into the next draw before they expose themselves to possible predators.

Evening trails follow the same principles, except deer move from higher to lower elevations and tend to keep the *wind at their backs* as they move toward preferred feeding locations. Nighttime trail activity tends to be along the tops of ridges and daytime activity tends to follow below the top of the ridge line.

I will devote an entire chapter to the subject of why, how, and in what circumstances deer use the wind behind them to their advantage. Please see the chapter entitled "Winds of Change".

Escape trails are erratic, lead from one security cover to the next, are short lived, don't necessarily follow the path of least resistance, but rather create the quickest and most protected escape route possible, with the least amount of visibility and greatest amount of cover.

If you study trail activity long enough you will find that a few trails are bi-directional (traveled on in both directions) but on most trails the majority if not all of the tracks are pointed in one direction, either to or from feeding or bedding areas. Or in the case of escape trails, toward or between security cover. You will also find that deer use different trails to arrive at and leave feeding and bedding locations.

When you jump a deer, remember its location and note its direction of travel. If you noticed it before it spooked, note what it was doing before you spooked it.

Another excellent technique used to decipher travel patterns is what I call "back trailing". This is done by following a specific deer track, or a general game trail in the opposite direction of travel, to discover what the animals were doing before they arrived at your reference point.

If time and light allow, it's a good idea to back trail the deer you finally shoot. It can provide you a wealth of valuable information.

If you are setting up on an evening stand, you want to specifically back track late afternoon trails which lead to your location to see where your quarry is bedding. Do this during mid- day and practice the appropriate scent limitation techniques discussed in the chapter entitled "Scents and Nonsense".

If you have established a potential tree stand location, are familiar with the area and have taken the appropriate scent elimination precautions, you may want to stay in the stand until after dark to determine nighttime deer activity. If you try this, don't alert the deer to your presence and only leave once you are sure that all of the deer have departed.

General trail analysis works best at feeding locations or natural corridors which direct or restrict travel to a more limited or confined area. Since deer do not tend to bed in groups and do not bed in the same area day after day, the activity patterns around bedding locations are very indistinct.

Deer will have an initial feeding area located about 100 to 300 yards from their bedding area, and then have numerous additional locations which may extend up to one or two miles away. They feed at these other spots during the evening, until just before daylight and then browse their way back to their beds in the morning.

Since a variety of foods are abundant and easily available, blacktails do not have to travel far to fill their stomachs, nor do they satisfy their appetite in one location. For this reason it is not typical to find lots of deep rutted trails leading from bedding to feeding locations.

Because the wind patterns change from hour to hour and day to day and food is abundant, *it is the wind and not the food sources which direct a deer's travel patterns.* Because of this, blacktails use a variety of trails to reach their destination. I have hunted some very specific areas for many years now, and on only two occasions have I seen the same large buck on two consecutive evening hunts. In all my years of hunting I have only once seen a large buck on more than one occasion before I decided to kill him, and I have only seen two large bucks on more than one occasion, over a period of consecutive hunting seasons.

I find that it takes at least two to three years of intensive study and analysis to "start" to understand the interrelationship of trails and deer habits in any chosen area of analysis. I have hunted in some areas up to 10 years now and I am still adding information to my list and finding new interrelationships between a deer's habits and his habitat.

WIND:

While you're scouting, try to discern prevailing wind directions under various weather conditions. Keep your own notes, but you can also gain information about the general wind direction in your area from the weather bureau. Keep in mind that topography and vegetation can dramatically direct and change the prevailing wind direction.

Also, do not forget the morning and evening thermals in your planning. Hot air rises and cool air falls. Creeks and lakes can also create their own form of thermal air movement. Creeks cool air and cause it to fall and lakes, depending on whether they are hotter or cooler than the surrounding forests, cause variations in wind direction.

Since a blacktails' direction of travel is determined by the direction of the wind and not the food source, it is very important to know what the predominant wind direction is in the area you plan to hunt. You should also record what the wind direction is like under varying weather situations, during different times of the day, and at different seasons of the year.

I have an area where I can guarantee that you will see deer when the wind is moving in a specific direction. I told my nephew this late one October afternoon, but he didn't believe me, until he was skinning out his buck an hour and a half later.

Learning wind patterns will allow you to position yourself at the appropriate spot at the appropriate time. It takes a lot of hard work and analysis to even begin to grasp the reason for the various movement patterns and the interrelationships of food, terrain, travel patterns and the prevailing air currents. Are you willing to "pay your dues?" If so, welcome to "The Crazy Blacktail Hunters Club." The only requirement for entry is to have an insatiable love for learning more and more about this majestic, elusive animal.

DEER BEDS:

When you locate a deer bed or beds, try to figure out why the deer bedded where they did. Consider visibility, time of use, weather and temperature, protection from predators, avenues of escape and wind direction. Remember the locations for future reference and mark them on your map.

Check to see how the deer entered and left the bed, possible visual blind spots, where you believe they may have come from in the morning and where their first stop might be in the evening.

Blacktails will generally not bed far from their preferred food sources and since their preferred food sources are numerous, most bedding areas will be from a few hundred yards up to a half mile from the first locations they choose to feed at.

In the summer deer look for cooler or shaded bedding locations and in the winter they choose areas which will provide some warmth or protection from the elements. Given similar cover, it's warmer up slope than in swales, creeks or hollows.

During the October hunting season check for beds on north, northeast or northwest slopes. Deer do not bed along creeks or in the bottom of gullies and similar situations so you don't need to waste your time there.

You might consider hiking, biking or driving your chosen hunting area during cold weather to locate the warmer areas and in turn make notes of cooler areas for early season use. It's surprising how quickly the temperature can change in a short distance.

If there is sign of other wildlife activity, then deer will be using the area also, but if the area seems devoid of animals then it most likely is. Don't waste your time there.

Instinct teaches mature bucks that predators such as bears, cougars and coyotes "scentralize" their hunting area and will cruise through known bedding locations and security cover to increase their chances of success.

A deer's most unfailing sense is their sense of smell and their most vulnerable area is the immediate area behind them. *For this reason bucks will bed so they can watch their back trail from a distance and will always use the prevailing wind and thick noisy cover behind them to warn them of danger on their immediate back trail. Typically they will also try to bed below the top of the ridge line so that they are covered by the prevailing winds from behind and the warming thermals from below. Except during the rut bucks will also bed together so that several sets of eyes, ears, and noses are covering all areas of concern, at all times!*

Photo credit: Chuck Bartlett

The secret to a bucks survival. Cover from behind and visibility to his back trail.

Photo credit: Boyd Iverson

Wind from behind and three sets of eyes and ears to cover the rest.

The oldest, or in some cases, the dominant buck will be the first to travel uphill in the morning and he will normally be bedded below the top of the ridge in the highest strategic position on the hill or at one of the upper points of a finger ridge where it begins to drop off more steeply.

In the morning deer will travel with the prevailing wind or morning down hill thermals, in their face or crosswise to their direction of travel, and will scent check the cover ahead of them for predators.

Deer have pre-determined bedding locations in mind as they leave their evening feeding locations and as they near these locations they will move even more slowly and carefully, watching, listening and using their sensitive sense of smell to detect any danger ahead. When they near the location where they intend to bed they will either move directly into the location, travel past this area and then turn and walk back into it or they will turn before they reach their preferred location (generally uphill and above the trail) and make a loop and travel with the wind behind them, back to this location. *But no matter how they enter their bedding area, they will always bed so that the wind is coming from behind them and there is thick protective cover at their back and visibility towards their original back trail.*

By this procedure they are able to watch their more distant back trail, while at the same time, using their sense of smell and hearing to catch the scent and sound of any predator who may try to sneak up on them from behind. The eyes check for danger at a distance, but the nose and ears, being the most infallible senses that a deer has, cover the immediate area behind them, which is their most vulnerable location.

The smaller bucks, does and fawns will come later and will bed lower on the hill. This creates an additional early alert system for any predator or hunter who comes from below.

At some point during the day, unless there is an over-riding prevailing wind, the sun's warming process will cause the warmer air to move upward; this will allow a buck to both scent and see the area below him but may leave his immediate backside unprotected, if the thermals overpower the prevailing wind direction.

I'm not sure exactly what a deer's reaction to this change in wind direction is, but I assume that with the changing wind direction he will get up and move, possibly feed near his security cover and then re-bed in a location where his eyes will watch below him, and the wind will again protect the area behind him.

Photo credit: Chuck Bartlett

Safe and Secure!

As temperatures begin to cool in the afternoon there will be a thermal reversal and the normal thermal currents will begin to head down hill. During this thermal reversal or the changing of the guards, deer will begin to travel down hill to their chosen feeding locations. But always be aware that prevailing winds can cancel out or change the normal thermal process.

I have found that blacktails in my area prefer to bed on hillsides and ridges intermixed with fir thickets, alder draws and tall ferns. As mentioned previously, the largest bucks will typically bed below the tops of these ridges. The lesser bucks and does will bed further down hill and act as a natural alarm system. Bucks will bed behind a handy clump of ferns or blown over tree roots, in the center of a heavy vine maple patch, or beneath the low hanging, protective branches of small fir trees. They prefer a location which provides protection and screening of their form, from the eyes of predators, but still allows them good visibility of the surroundings.

In these type of locations they have good visibility below, can catch the scent and sound of approaching danger from behind and cannot be seen or approached quietly from below. One glimpse, sound, or scent of a hunter or other predator and they're immediately alert. They will then stay concealed, slowly sneak out undetected, or if danger is close or they feel that they have been spotted they may noisily break forth from their sanctuary.

Mature bucks prefer the silent escape and will only burst out of hiding as a last resort. But even then they will have their escape trails established so as to provide the greatest amount of screening between them and their enemies.

Study how any beds you discover are situated so that when you see other similar situations you will find the deer in its bed rather than just the signs of its presence.

When you jump a deer from its bed, note the direction of travel, which trail it used and the prevailing wind direction. *Consistently successful hunters are observers, note takers, and analyzers. Figuring out and out-foxing the animal is what the hunt's about!* An easy animal taken without any analysis or prior preparation is almost anti-climatic.

TRACKS:

Study all of the tracks you find to see what you can discover about the animal who made them and why and when they were made. If tracks enter a feeding location from the downhill side, then the deer passed through in the morning hours. If the tracks enter on the uphill side, the animal fed there in the evening.

A fresh track will be clear and distinct, not glazed over, hard or dry. It is important to be able to know how old a track is so you can decide the time of day the deer are using a particular trail, bed, or feeding spot.

If you find a particularly large track which might indicate, at the least, a large-bodied deer, check it out to see if it has any special characteristics by which you can identify it when you see it again. Many times the hooves on an old deer will be cut or broken in such a manner as to make them easily identifiable.

Even though my heart starts beating rapidly every time I see a large deer track, and we as hunters will always judge the size of a "bucks" antlers by the size of its track, we must always remember that just because the track is large and deeply imprinted into the ground does not necessarily mean that the deer's antlers are of a similar size or even that the deer has antlers. By studying all of the sign we can make some pretty good assumptions but we can only be sure when we see the deer standing in its tracks!

The second heaviest buck I shot, only sported a respectable but not overly large three point rack. Genetics and nutrients are more important than body weight when it comes to antler size.

Buck tracks are generally wider and larger. A buck's front hooves are longer than their rear hooves and a mature buck puts more pressure on the rear portion of his hooves, causing the toes to be more splayed, with the toes separated and pointed outward. A mature buck's rear hooves usually fall to the inside and short of the impression left by his front hooves. Also since mature bucks are heavier in the front section of their body, their front hooves will make deeper imprints than the rear hooves. A buck's dew claws are closer to the hooves on the front feet, so there is more of a chance for the dew claws of a buck to show, in a normal walking situation. Both doe and buck tracks may show dew claw indentation while running, while walking in soft areas, or while climbing up or sliding down hills.

If you find a group of tracks together and a larger track that is off to one side and tends to make better use of shadows and available cover, then these tracks would probably belong to a buck. A buck's track also tends to show a more irregular travel pattern than a doe's.

A buck will urinate ahead of his rear feet, with a more direct spray which can easily be identified if there is snow on the ground. They will also drag their rear feet, which again shows up easily when there is snow on the ground but not so easily at most other times.

A doe's tracks are usually smaller and more heart-shaped, and because a doe carries most of her weight in the rear section of her anatomy, there will be less splay at the toes of the front hooves and more spacing at the toes of the rear hooves. A doe's rear tracks tend to fall on top of, or slightly outside of, her front tracks and the toes on her front

Photo credit: Boyd Iverson

Small rubs, small bucks!

hooves tend to dig in deeper than her rear hooves. Does urinate between their rear feet with a less direct spray.

When you're following tracks don't walk on the trail, but rather three or four feet to a few yards off trail, on the down wind side.

With the exception of the rut a large bucks' tracks will rarely be seen on well-used trails. He prefers to travel where there is more cover and where he can watch or scent check the more heavily traveled routes at a safe distance. But when the rut or actually the "pre-rut" begins, the well used trails, which previously were barren of noticeably large deer tracks, will show evidence of the wide splayed tracks of running "bucks" etched deeply into the rain soaked ground. This is a site to truly gladden and excite the heart of any dyed-in-the-wool blacktail hunter. The hunt is on!!!! Rifle or bow ready, mind alert!!

DROPPINGS:

A deer will leave approximately 12 different piles of droppings in a day's time. Deer are most apt to defecate soon after they get up from bedding, while feeding or as they first leave a feeding location. Note where you find droppings and ask yourself what they tell you.

Fresh droppings will generally be soft and shiny, runny, or hard depending on the food eaten. Hard firm pellets would indicate that the deer are browsing on woody scrubs and soft or running droppings indicate that they are feeding on grasses or softer foods. Weather can affect the exterior surface and therefore affect our analysis. To be sure of the age you should gently squeeze them. If they are hard and brittle inside then they are at least a day or two old, depending on the temperature in the area. If, on the other hand, they are uniformly soft throughout, then they are only a few hours old. If they are warm or even steaming and the tracks are walking and not running, get your rifle or bow ready, you're about to get the thrill of your life!

It is believed by deer researchers, that buck droppings are generally larger in size and are usually clumped together in one large clump or several small clumps. Doe droppings on the other hand are usually in the form of individual loose pellets or clusters of individual pellets.

RUBS:

You can learn a lot about deer activity by looking at rubs. Blacktails typically rub smaller evergreen trees in the summer months to remove velvet and establish territorial boundaries. During the rut smaller bucks will use a single small evergreen tree or deciduous tree, but the larger bucks generally use larger deciduous trees. The bigger the buck the bigger the tree. I've only seen one instance where a large buck rubbed his antlers on evergreen trees during the rut and in this case he attacked a cluster of several trees in a small clearing. This buck basically massacred all of the trees and left them with rubbed off bark and many broken branches.

Most rubs are made prior to the actual breeding time and are done during the time when the bucks are first getting excited, what we call the pre-rut. Once a large number of does are ready to breed the number of rubs will diminish.

Bucks will rub trees in the same general area year after year and will sometimes use the same specific tree several years in a row. I know of one especially large, uniquely shaped tree, which has fresh scars etched into its bark every year.

Early spring, before the leaves are back on the trees and shrubs, is an excellent time to look for last season's rubs, as they stand out clearly in this "unleafed environment."

When you're looking for rubs it's a good idea to get down on your knees to see the woods from a deer's perspective. Make good use of your binoculars to fully scan your surroundings. This also gives you good practice for the fall hunting season. You can reasearch the potential core areas at this time of the year without the fear of disturbing the area and affecting your hunt. Check the pattern of rubs and trails to determine the why and where-fors of deer travel. Unless the habitat changes, the animals will use these same areas next fall during the hunting season. It's also a safe time to choose potential stand locations, determine your line of sight and do miscellaneous pruning and clearing.

Look for these rub lines along travel lanes on the sides of ridges, in cross over swales or gullies, along the edges of small creeks, along drainage ravines, on the edges of feeding locations, in dense protective cover near feeding areas and along old overgrown logging roads, especially if they

Photo credit: Boyd Iverson

This is a rub worth checking out!

are grown over with alder or similar deciduous vegetation along their edges.

Mark all of these rub locations on your topo and aerial photo and then try to decipher the cause and effect of animals habits and movement patterns.

When you find rubs, note which side of the tree the rub is on. As a general rule, if the rub is on the uphill side of the tree it was made in the evening when the buck was coming down to feed. If the rub is on the downhill side of the tree, it was made in the morning when the buck was traveling from feeding to bedding locations. A line of rubs will show direction of travel and also the specific breeding territory of a buck. *Most rubs are made near to of after dark or in the early morning hours.*

I've personally only seen two bucks actually rubbing trees. One was early in the A.M. and the other was very late in the evening. *These rubs will show you what type of bucks are in the area, but will not necessarily give you a shot, simply by set-*

ting up a stand near the rub. On the other hand I have heard about a lot of hunters taking bucks near or approaching rubbed trees.

Try to find out what other information you can discover by studying a buck rub. Did the buck have eye guards and if so, how long? (Shown by scars in the middle of the rubbed tree) How wide were his antlers, as noted by any marks along side the tree. How old is the rub? (Is the color fresh or faded? Is the sap still running?) Is it a summer velvet removing or mock sparing early territorial determination rub or a rub made during the rut? Are there other fresh rubs nearby which would indicate the territory of a particular buck? Are there other old rubs nearby which would indicate a regular breeding area? What trees do the bucks in your area prefer to rub? In the area I hunt they prefer alder or ash. To my knowledge blacktails do not make scrapes, at least in all my years of hunting and time spent in the woods I have never found one.

Photo credit: Boyd Iverson

This is the most active rub I've ever found. This rub was made by the buck I messed up on, during the late muzzle loader season.

CORE AREAS:

Telemetric studies show that deer generally stay within a specific home range, but that they spend a disproportionate amount of their time in specific areas of their home range which we will call "hot spots" or "core areas". They spend about 90% of their time on 10% to 20% of their home range. A large buck's core area may be as small as a 100 yards across, but is usually five to 10 acres in size.

As hunting pressure intensifies, this core area becomes smaller and smaller and must provide the buck with the essentials of security cover, food and moisture. When you pin-point these locations, your chances of success will be much greater. These same spots will produce large bucks year after year unless the habitat is changed dramatically.

Telemetric studies have also shown that when deer encounter heavy hunting pressure they do not leave, as is commonly believed, but rather they simply decrease their daytime and even evening activity and stay very close to home. Their "home" is usually situated in heavy, somewhat inaccessible cover, with multiple escape routes and additional security cover close at hand. Studies have shown that the older the buck, the more sedentary is his behavior. During heavy hunting pressure a buck's *daytime* travel area may be limited to an area as small as 100 by 100 yards, and blacktails have been known to stay in a small patch of heavy cover for several days at a time, to avoid hunters. The bucks that survive are the ones which move the least during the daylight hours.

CLEAR CUTS:

I'm not sure what the fascination with new clear cuts is, but as soon as the loggers are done and sometimes even before, hunters are drawn to them like magnets to metal. They sit at the edges in eager anticipation. They tromp through and around them and a few brave souls even venture a few hundred yards into the woods surrounding them, but generally to no avail. Usually these efforts produce nothing more than tracks or an occasional younger deer.

Sure, there is a lot of deer activity in new clear cuts but most, if not all of it, is during the off-season or after dark. Only the young, the fool-hardy and the soon to be dead stay until daylight or arrive before dusk. During normal rifle seasons most respectable bucks are long gone by shooting light and do not enter the openings until well after legal shooting light. You might catch a big buck here the first few mornings of the season or during the pre-rut, but it is the exception rather than the rule.

The principle exceptions to this are clear cuts which are at least two or three years old, are not easily accessible and therefore not hunted heavily or have lower overgrown benches which are not visible from roadways or high vantage points. The other exception to this principle would be during the early archery season when the bucks are still in their "velvet protecting and high protein consumption mode." *Clear cuts can and do produce trophy bucks but the most successful way to hunt them is to hunt the peripheral areas early or late, rather than the clearing itself.*

One year loggers clear cut a patch of timber near where I used to hunt. This immediately brought a hoard of hunters into the area, like bees to honey. After this occurred, I hunted for a solid week and saw only four or five small deer tracks crossing any of the common travel corridors that I used to access my hunting area. The deer had simply bottled up until the commotion was over.

HOMEWORK:

At the end of each day transfer your written field notes to your map or onto a clear mylar overlay which will fit on top of either your topo or your aerial photo. This enables you to visualize the deer activity pattern and will help you locate the hot spots. Remember though, that these hot spots can, and do, change during the different seasons, due to food choices, weather conditions, breeding habits and yes, hunting pressure.

At least once every year go over your previous years' notes to see what new pieces of the puzzle you can put together. I have learned much valuable information by going back over my old notes and observations.

A nice way to keep your hunting information current or an idea to use when researching a new area is to get a standard aerial photo, scan it on a computer and then enlarge it as needed, to encompass your specific hunting area. Make copies. Carry one of these into the field with you and keep one at home for updating and recording notes and observations.

You can also scan your topo map or you can buy one of the new computer programs which allow you to print topo maps of your area. These computer topographic programs can show you elevation changes along any trail you choose, allow you to plot trails and make notes you want on the computer and then print out the maps to take along with you.

Make sure you know the scale on your aerial or topo maps so you can correlate distances. The new GPS units also can be used very effectively to mark or find areas of interest on your topo maps.

Photos of Reader's Bucks

Bob Gerding
Western Oregon

At left:
Shannon Gerding
Western Oregon

Below:
Dean Trent
Western Oregon

At right:
Tom Carley
Western Oregon

Below:
Bob Robb
Southern Oregon

Cameron Hanes
Western Oregon

Todd Graham
Western Oregon

Phil Hunter
Western Oregon

Todd Wilkinson
Western Oregon

At left:
Curt Brace
Western Oregon

Below:
Todd Wilkinson
Western Oregon

Larry and Joann Brace. True togetherness. Sharing a photo with a
very large buck.
Western Oregon

Ken Barr
Western Oregon

Tom Carley
Western Oregon

Shannon Gerding
Western Oregon

At left:
Joann Brace
Western Oregon

Below:
Phil Hunter
Western Oregon

At right:
Jay Marcott
Cascade Buck

Below:
Bobby McClory
Western Oregon

From left to right: Justin Gerding, Jenny Gerding, Jason Gerding, Fran Gerding. Hunting: A family tradition!
Western Oregon

Rod and Ryan Hoffstot: Father and son hunting partners!
Western Oregon

Jay Marcott
Cascade Buck

Kieth Julian
Western Oregon

At left:
Fran Gerding
Western Oregon

Below:
Cameron Hanes
Western Oregon

Curt Brace
Western Oregon

Chapter 8

The Ultimate Challenge
Still Hunting

A mericans are always in a hurry and we carry this fast-paced mentality into the woods with us. Because of this many of us are "still hunting" instead of correctly and successfully still hunting.

As we leave our busy world and ease into a big buck's domain we need to acclimatize ourselves to a buck's life style of "slow down and live". Take a few minutes and let your senses adjust to this new environment. Learn to blend. *Forget the fast-paced world you've left, slip into the slow-paced life of the woods, and follow the natural pattern of animal movement.* A good rule to hunt by is: never move faster than the pace of an undisturbed deer!

An old quote says it well, "Happiness is not found at the end of the trail, but along the way." A hunter should learn to move with the expectation that at any second he will see, or better yet, that he will be seen by a buck. The only way to avoid detection is to move slower, think smarter, blend better, and observe as intently as the game you pursue.

Many times we move with the expectation of seeing a deer around the next bend or over the next ridge and we are always in a hurry to get to new territory. Reverse this expectation and substitute caution for speed and your success ratio will increase. *The negative affects of moving too quickly are cumulative. The faster you move the more noise you make, the less that you hear and the less details you see, while at the same time, you're alerting the game with a variety of danger signals.*

Photo credit: Boyd Iverson

Smaller buck is obviously alerted. Neck upright, eyes and ears alert!

If you enjoy seeing the white flags of disturbed deer don't change but if you'd prefer to see what the front end of a deer looks like, you need to *slow it down!!*

As long as we check wind direction, deer are first alerted to our presence by unnatural sound or movement. When you remain motionless you become "invisible" to a deer's ears as well as its eyes. Any quick upward movements of your arms or hands are especially alarming and quickly and easily seen, as this is the universal motion of alarmed birds and game animals. *Any predator pursued game knows that any flushed bird or quick movement signals danger or alarm.*

To help avoid detection you should move slowly with minimal arm and body movement and walk with a light step. Don't just flop your foot down, but rather roll it slowly onto the ground, keeping your weight on one foot as you step ahead with your other foot and then gradually putting your weight on this new foot, a little at a time, all the while testing for invisible sticks or twigs, before transferring your full weight to the ground.

Footwear is vitally important. The boots you wear should have comparatively soft soles. Heavy, stiff soled hiking boots, ski boots, and old military boots have no place in still hunting. Use boots with as soft and sensitive a sole as is comfortable. Many an undetected twig has snapped beneath the sole of a heavy hunting boot and so allowed a big buck to live another year.

Also since we are talking about boots, it's very important to mention that if your boots don't fit you correctly, you won't be able to hunt effectively.

With your hunting socks on, you should be able to put one finger behind your heel. Another way to test the fit is to stand on a steep slope or on a board placed at the bottom of your stairs and see if your toes hit the end of your boots. If your toes touch the end of your boots then they're too short. Also, and at this point I may sound like your mother, keep your toe nails clipped. It should go without saying that you need to break in your boots prior to the hunting season.

As you proceed try to create the "illusion of non-movement". Move in a fluid non jerky pattern with no abrupt or quick actions. Avoid sudden head or hand motions and keep your arms at your sides or at waist level in front of you.

In every case unless a deer is already alarmed and moving, slow movements will give you a better chance for a shot.Do your best to become part of the landscape in sight, sound and scent. (Scent will be covered in the chapter entitled "Scents and Nonsense").

Quick jerky movements immediately spook, or at the least alarm wildlife. Visualize how easily even our eyes pick up the quick action of a bird or squirrel in the woods, versus say, the slow gliding motion of a snake or bobcat. Imitate the actions of a predator and study how a buck who has survived several years in the woods protects himself from these predators. Try to discover a deer's weak points and areas of vulnerability.

Chuck Bartlett, the photographer who has supplied most of the great live blacktail photos for this book says, *that any more than three steps in succession will alert an animal to mans presence.* It will not necessarily alarm them, but they will now be on alert and direct all of their senses to discover what caused this unnatural sound intrusion. I guarantee you that Chuck does not obtain the fantastic, natural, unalarmed, photos of blacktails which he has taken, by alerting them to his presence. So I for one will listen to his wisdom.

Watch and learn from the game itself, or better yet, the actions of the predators who hunt them. *Move cautiously, taking advantage of all available cover, both visual (vegetation,* shadows, etc.) and auditory (a jet flying overhead, the wind blowing in the trees, the squawking of a distant jay or crow, other noisy hunters, etc.). Whenever possible move when the sounds of your activity will be disguised by these other disturbances.

When you stop be sure that your human outline is screened or camouflaged by natural vegetation and your face and body is shaded. The importance of staying in the shadows was again illustrated to me on a recent hunt. I was still hunting and came upon two large bucks feeding in a comparatively open area, at a distance of no more than 25 to 35 yards. I spotted them before they were aware of my presence and I watched them feed for several minutes. During this time they looked directly at me on numerous occasions, with no sign of recognition or alarm, yet I was not dressed in camo and was not even shielded by any sight obscuring vegetation.

But I was standing in the shadows rather than in the sun light. Finally after about 10 minutes they started moving away and I slowly followed at an increasing distance. At one point I had to cross a small sunlit area and this was my downfall.

I moved only when the bucks' heads were down or they were looking away, and I was totally immobile when they again looked in my direction. But with my new position covered in sunlight, the bucks immediately spotted me and bounded away even though at this time they were 50 to 80 yards away.

The shadows had naturally screened and protected me from discovery but the sun had spot-lighted my distinct human form and shiny face.

Camouflage those areas of your body which are the most visible and are involved in the most amount of unnatural movement, i.e., your hands and your face. A white shiny face and white hands flashing in the sunlight are a dead giveaway for you and a lifesaver for many a buck. I find face masks to be confining and affect my vision so while still hunting I prefer to use camo paints or simply a piece of charcoal or charred piece of cork to darken my face and hands. If you are bow hunting you may prefer to use full camouflage but a rifle hunter, for safety reasons, should use camouflage only on his hands, face, and possibly his pants.

YOUR MOVEMENTS AND ACTIONS ARE MUCH MORE IMPORTANT THAN THE COLOR OF THE CLOTHES YOU WEAR, except that it is important to wear clothing with large broken color patterns rather than a solid color.

Recent studies indicate that game animals are not color blind as previously believed. These studies show that big game animals see colors but they see them differently than us. Big game animals see the colors blue and grey very well but they do not see oranges and reds *as* oranges and reds. Given their ability to detect the color blue, it would obviously not be a good idea to wear blue clothing and especially blue jeans! It is believed that yellow, brown, gray, red, and orange are all seen as a shade of yellow. Also, it is believed that if you remove the fluorescent glow from fluorescent colors by washing them in the appropriate laundry products, deer will simply see fluorescent colors as a shade of yellow also.

Because of the way big game animals eyes' are structured they are very sensitive to ultraviolet light, especially in dim light situations, and this light is seen as a bright bluish glow. Brighteners or whiteners used in many commercial laundry detergents work by increasing the amount of UV reflected from clothing, which creates the same bright bluish glow which big game animals are most sensitive to.

Make sure and wash your clothes in unscented detergents which do not have added whiteners or brighteners. If you do use fluorescent camouflage clothing or have washed any of your hunting clothes in laundry detergents with whiteners or brighteners, use one of the UV blocking sprays or detergents before you go hunting.

To be consistently successful we need to use all of our senses to the maximum. Learn to distinguish individual sounds and decipher what you're actually hearing. In our busy society, we are constantly bombarded by a multitude of sounds and stimuli so we have trained our minds to block out sounds to avoid confusion, rather than to sort out and identify them. Take for example people who live by railroads or busy freeways. After a while, they don't seem to notice the disturbance. In actuality, they do hear the sound but the brain does not register or react to it. *But you should remember that every sound in the woods has meaning!!!*

Since humans no longer need to survive by using our predator instincts, these abilities have diminished from lack of use. But if someone told us that there were $1,000 dollar bills placed in the woods, we would soon learn to distinguish the color and shape of those bills! *We can retrain our senses to be sensitive to nature and to distinguish and locate our quarry in its natural environment.* (This subject is covered later in the section entitled "Seeing is Believing".)

Be flexible and sensitive to changing weather and wind direction. *Prevailing wind direction and thermals should always be a factor in your direction of travel.* Remember that the normal thermal air currents follow the sun, up in the morning and down in the evening. These thermals can and will be overridden by prevailing winds but on a calm day with little to no wind the thermals will control air movement and should control your movement. If it is windy, wind direction tends to be up hill or across hill.

Photo credit: Chuck Bartlett

Always hunt into, or crossways to the wind, because scent and sound are both carried by the wind. Remember, that deer will generally be bedded with their backs or their rear ends facing the prevailing wind while their eyes search for danger on approaching trails. Deer tend to be more concerned with visual "downhill danger" and use their hearing and sense of smell to protect them from potential danger from above. Sound travels and is amplified as it travels upward, and visibility in general is normally better from above. Because of this, try to follow trails that are equal in elevation to, or that criss-cross *above*, where you expect to locate game.

On a finger ridge coming off a main ridge, bucks tend to bed within a few hundred yards of the point where the ridge drops down steeply at the end to allow them to see in both directions and can bail off either side when alarmed. On a standard ridge bucks tend to bed somewhat below the top of the ridge.

Here's a key point to remember! In steep mountainous terrain, concentrate on hunting on or slightly above the various benches which show up on your topo map. The major bedding activity will be above or below these benches and the major feeding activity will be on these benches!

Keep in mind that bedded dear will be facing and looking in the opposite direction or cross wise to the prevailing wind direction, and that they will be bedded along the side hill or along, or at the end, of a finger ridge.

Use a wind indicator tied to the end of your bow or rifle such as a piece of frayed unwaxed dental floss. If it's dry, a marabou feather works best since it will show the direction of even the slightest air changes. The use of powder is good to detect especially light air patterns, but it takes movement on the hunter's part to use this type of product, and the less unnatural movement the better. On a cold, humid day, watching your own breath is the best and the easiest way to check wind direction.

A BUCK'S SURVIVAL TACTICS:

The only time a buck travels at a steady walk is when he is frightened or deep in the rut with some female on his mind. If you've ever watched an undisturbed buck as he's traveling through the woods or as he approaches a feeding location, you will notice that he takes only one or two cautious steps at a time. Then he stops, with his body fully or partially screened by brush, the overhanging branches of a tree, high ferns, or any other convenient vegetation. He will stand this way for as long as it takes for his senses to tell him all is well, before he proceeds onward. Unlike humans, he has no timetable to keep. *His ultimate concern is survival and his survival necessitates stealth, not speed.*

His moist, black nose is active, constantly testing the air or the trail he is traveling on, for familiar reassuring or unfamiliar and therefore alarming, scents. He may possibly browse on a succulent leaf or sprout and then continue to survey his immediate surroundings.

His radar-like ears are attentive, swiveling first one direction and then the next, listening for any stray sound, while his large dark eyes are intently searching his surroundings for any stray movement. If there is more than one buck, they will be looking in different directions and even have their ears funnelled in opposite directions. If a buck joins another buck who is already bedded, the new buck will bed so that he watches what the first buck cannot.

If two bucks are traveling together into a feeding spot the younger animal will always enter first. If they're proceeding to a bedding area in the morning the opposite will be true; the oldest or the dominant buck will always be ahead.

Deer know what's going on ahead of them long before they actually reach their chosen location. I have watched undisturbed bucks which are approaching a feeding area take 20 to 30 minutes to cover 20 to 30 yards. They pause at the periphery and continue to survey their domain once more before they timidly poke their noses out of the protective cover. Then they still take two to three additional minutes to proceed from the exposure of their inquisitive noses and searching eyes to the exposure of their bodies.

If anything seems to be out of place, they quickly and quietly fade from sight and melt back into their protective environment. *It doesn't take much to alert a smart old buck. Even the fact that there are none of the other normal natural sounds or small game activity, is enough to make him cautious.* Sometimes a bucks disappearance happens so unobtrusively that we begin to doubt that we ever saw anything in the first place.

If you're still hunting and a mature buck is alerted to your presence, he will move quietly out of your path, or more likely, will stay where he is and carefully monitor your progress, anticipate your arrival, and wait for your departure. He prefers to creep and slink rather than run. Smart old bucks have learned that they're very vulnerable

Photo credit: Chuck Bartlett

Ever get the feeling that you're being watched?

to other predators, besides the one they're escaping from, when they are running, since their senses cannot function adequately in this situation. So mature bucks do not run far when they feel that they must escape quickly.

Listen the next time you jump a mature animal. Usually four or five bounds is all you hear and then silence. A younger deer will make more noise and for a longer period of time. A big buck will run only as a last resort, if you're "too" close or he thinks that he's been seen.

While mule deer tend to run uphill when spooked, I find that blacktails tend to travel down or side hill when spooked.

If you are fortunate enough to spot a bedded or hidden buck and he is already aware of your presence but feels that he is hidden, do not create direct eye contact until you are ready to shoot and use no abrupt or quick movements to get your rifle or bow ready.

TACTICS AND TECHNIQUES:

Still hunting is in most cases a one person sport. Generally two hunters do not work effectively together. There are certain situations though, when both hunters know the country and each other's hunting techniques, where a two-person still hunt can be extremely effective in taking game.

There are two techniques to be used in this type of procedure, to match the two different big buck's survival tactics. The first survival tactic is for the buck to get up slightly ahead of the first still hunter and then circle around behind and down wind of this hunter or let the hunter pass and then get up and monitor his presence by sight, scent and sound. The second survival tactic is for the buck to slowly and silently move out ahead of the hunter.

If you choose to still hunt with a partner under this first scenario then the first hunter should always be ahead and the second hunter, down wind or cross wind and behind the first hunter. Both hunters in this situation should be hunting into or cross ways to the wind. How far behind is decided by the terrain and the thickness of the cover. Both hunters should hunt slowly and silently just as if they were solo still hunting. The second hunter is the one most likely to get a shot in this situation, since a buck will circle behind and downwind of the first hunter and will be up and watching the first hunter depart. While the buck is concentrating on what the first hunter is doing the second hunter gets the shot.

The second technique is used to get those bucks who choose to move out ahead of the hunter. In this case the first hunter sets up *with the wind in his face*, at a good viewing spot or potential escape trail, 20 to 30 minutes before the second hunter begins to work through the security cover. The second hunter proceeds into the cover *with the wind at his back,* so that his scent is blown into the cover he is working. He should slowly zig zag back and forth through the cover just like he was still hunting by himself. He might get the shot, but it is usually the first hunter in this situation who gets the action.

If positioned correctly, any bucks moving out ahead of the second hunter, using the prevailing winds to keep track of his actions, will come under the sights of the first hunter. This style of hunting is more like a series of orchestrated ambushes, than joint still hunting. Each hunter should alternate positions until successful.

An intimate knowledge, by both of the hunters, of the habitat, wind currents, and trail activity is needed to make this technique consistently successful. Remember though, that you can't push deer or force them to go in a particular direction, but you can set up to cover the direction you naturally think they will travel.

Greg Miller, a very successful whitetail hunter believes that bucks specifically move out of security cover when they are disturbed, with the wind at their backs, to keep scent contact with their most immediate concern, which is the hunter on their back trail. They use their eyes and ears to scout the cover ahead of them.

If both hunters know the territory well and know where security or bedding areas are located and the associated escape trails they can post one hunter on potential escape trails while the other partner carefully and slowly still hunts through likely cover. Again be sure that the first hunters scent is not being blown into the security cover or into the trail which he is watching and be sure that the animals are not aware of his viewing location by sight, scent or sound.

Since the idea is to cause game to move out of protective cover it is best if the still hunter works with the wind at his back and blowing into the cover he is hunting. Obviously in this situation the two hunters need to trade off positions during the day.

These still hunting techniques are most successful during mid-day when the deer are bedded down or secured in their area of preferred cover.

But in the majority of situations having another hunter along takes the flexibility out of adjusting to the specific circumstances you discover in the woods. *With a partner you must set up a "time and place-destination" and you tend to lose your awareness, in the urgency of arriving at a predetermined site at a specific time.* I have yet to find a partner who I can effectively still hunt with.

I personally do not still hunt bedding areas in familiar habitat. I find that if hunters continually disturb a large buck's resting area, he will become even more secretive and reclusive and may become totally nocturnal in his feeding and bedding habits.

The less disturbed a large buck is, the better your chances of catching him early or late when he is mobile and more vulnerable. I also do not still hunt bedding areas because the buck has all the advantages. Even though I may have time to place a quick shot as he moves from his bed, I do not have adequate time to analyze antler size before shooting and would rather post up on a trail leading to or leaving the bucks security cover.

The best still hunting conditions are during a light, misty rain, with the wind blowing in a constant direction, or right after a heavy rain that has continued for most of the day and stops an hour or two before the end of legal shooting light. The rain softens noisy leaves and branches and causes a steady drip from vegetation, which helps muffle human noise. Also, the grayness caused by the low cloud cover causes deer to head for bedding locations later in the morning and also to come out to feed earlier in the evening. Heavy rains, and gusty, unstable, wind conditions on the other hand, cause deer to be very jumpy and nervous. In these types of weather conditions still hunting through heavily timbered habitat is a good bet.

Since deer expect movement on trails, always walk on established deer trails, and time your movement with the natural movement pattern of deer in the area. This is where deer expect movement and established trails make for the most quiet travel. *Only a hunter or a badly scared or wounded deer will travel noisily off trail. In the morning, hunt trails leading from feeding to bedding locations and in the evening, reverse your approach.*

Like all rules there are exceptions to these rules which might produce a deer under correct circumstances. Sometimes you will reach an area where quiet is next to impossible. If you're a rifle hunter this might be a time to try to use noise to your advantage. I've used this a couple of times to my success.

In each situation the trail I was following came to an extremely noisy brush patch, with no good chance for a quiet approach. So instead of making a series of sound alerts, I quickly plowed through the brush, immediately stopped, screened my human form with available vegetation, and stayed that way for several minutes. In both cases,

I broke the nerves of bucks who heard the commotion but could not pin-point my location or identify what I was, became nervous and broke cover to escape. This was the last mistake they made!

Walk around openings, not through them and move in shaded locations, not open sunlight. Peek over ridges and carefully glass the opposite side before proceeding onward. Screen your human outline with available vegetation or cross over at low spots. Make as little unnatural movement as possible and make your movements slow. Especially avoid any quick upward movements of your hands or arms. Visualize what your reaction is when you jump a grouse or a covey of quail, as they rise in an upward flutter of wings and scattered feathers.

Some sort of loose camouflage material sewed under the arms, which fills in the void left when we lift our arms might be a good idea.

To lessen the chance of any game animals identifying the sounds you are making as those of a human, rather than

Photo credit: Boyd Iverson

"You've been had!"

one of the woods animals, *vary your speed and your gait, pausing often to search out the surrounding terrain.* By moving slowly and intently searching your hunting area you limit your visual and sound intrusion and your slow approach may cause a buck to think he's been discovered, so that he moves and exposes himself or you may discover some movement, color, or form which materializes into the buck of your dreams.

In still hunting, *the hunter must always be prepared, with his mind and bow or rifle ready.* He must move slowly and cautiously, do more looking than walking and travel with an animal-like uneven tempo. *Humans are the only things in the woods who walk with a steady even gait.*

Take short steps so that less weight is transferred to the ground and you can stop in mid-stride if needed. *Never step on anything you can step over.* Nothing is so awkward as being caught by an animal when you're in mid-stride with one foot on the ground and the other dangling precariously in the air. If you get caught in this position by an alert game animal you're basically had!! You can very, very slowly lower the raised leg but you'll most likely lose the contest. I know because I've been in this situation on several occasions!

SOUND AND SCENT CONTAINMENT AND ANALYSIS:

As you travel through the woods do not broadcast your presence, and be as nondisruptive as possible. Do not use your bare hands to move or part branches unless it is absolutely necessary. This increases motion and thus visibility and also leaves a human scent trail which a deer will readily pick up when it travels on the same trail. *Let the bushes slide quietly off of your body as they would off the hide of a deer. Deer work on the principle of hearing, identification and reaction. If the sound they hear is categorized as "natural" then the reaction part of their response is postponed and we are able to outwit their senses.*

God wisely engineered deer ears so that they are able to rotate in varying directions independent of each other. This enables them to zero in on any noise disturbances. In addition to this they have about seven or eight times the hearing capacity of humans and their hearing is structured so that they are more sensitive to close sounds, rather than distant sounds, even though the distant sounds may be very loud. I've seen deer almost jump out of their skins when a noisy leaf lands nearby or become instantly alert when I've made even the slightest unnatural sound. But when a distant rifle shot echos across the hillside, they pay little to no attention.

We need to get rid of all items that go bang, clank and thump, in the woods. Carefully analyze all of your hunting paraphernalia before you go hunting to see what needs to be "quietized", left at home, or replaced. Get rid of, or apply protective coverings to any items which might betray your presence to a deer's constantly searching ears.

Cover metal objects such a belt buckles or zipper pulls with a rubber coating like that used on hand tools or replace metal zipper pulls with leather. Don't use nylon backpacks or gaiters, or any items with noisy velcro openers or noisy canvas or nylon covers. Replace metal connections on gun slings with buckskin thongs. Don't leave loose items in your pockets that might bang together. Don't wear rings or jewelry, and leave your keys or any noisy items back at your car.

When you are still hunting you should dress the part. Wear soft, sensitive clothing and footwear. Don't wear noisy denim, nylon or synthetic clothing. Branches brushing against wool, polar-tec or similar products and the rubbing together of the legs of wool, polar-tec, worsterlon, saddle cloth, or any of the new quiet hunting pants are sounds similar to those made by branches brushing against a deer's soft hide. Branches brushing against nylon, new denim jeans or many of the other garments carelessly worn by hunters is an easily distinguishable and immediately alarming, unnatural sound.

If it's raining and you must wear rain gear don't use any of the cheap plastic varieties, and cover the rain gear with soft outer garments or purchase some of the new quiet rain gear. The day pack or fanny pack you use should also be made from one of the new sound sensitive materials.

As you are hunting keep track of important information such as direction of deer activity on the trails, natural corridors and geographic features which centralize deer movement, food sources, buck rubs, bedding locations, secluded pockets which might offer protection during a bad storm, trail intersection points and other information which is vital to helping you understand the general pattern of deer movement and activity in your area.

To be successful you must learn to categorize every sound, use all of your senses to their maximum, and remember that every sound has a source, so don't move or relax until you have determined that source! TAKE NOTHING YOU HEAR FOR GRANTED! No big game animal nor predator moves without some sound! Learn to interpret woods sounds and listen to the signals of other wildlife. Don't ignore nature's signals. Squirrels and jays are the tattletales of nature. When they're talking it's because somebody or something has alarmed them. "CHECK IT OUT". Practice distinguishing and identifying the various noises that you hear. When I first started hunting I missed shots at a couple of very large bucks because I assumed that no deer could be making so much noise. I let my guard down and was rewarded with the wide antlers and rear end of quickly departing bucks. I don't assume anything any more!

Several times I have spotted bucks because I heard them before they heard me, or at least before they determined that the sound they heard was something they needed to fear.

On one occasion I had just settled down to watch an interesting opening for a few minutes, when I heard the sound of an approaching deer off to my left and slightly behind me. I slowly twisted around to watch for its approach but I did not get my rifle ready. This was a big mistake!! When the three point buck came down the trail only a few yards from me, he spotted my movement as I raised my rifle, and froze, with his neck screened by a small fir tree. Needless to say, I drilled the fir tree dead center. The splinters from the tree peppered the buck's face and he went sailing pell-mell in the opposite direction, a frantic look of shock and amazement on his face, but happy to be alive! I'll always remember the look on that buck's face.

I once saw the rear end of a small doe that looked exactly like a rock. The rock seemed out of place in its grass covered surroundings, so I put my binoculars on it. It wasn't until the doe lifted her head that I knew that the "rock" was a deer. *Never be in a hurry to cover more territory. Worry instead, about covering thoroughly your immediate environment! Carry good quality binoculars and use them! Hunt as if you have already spotted a buck and are attempting to sneak up on him.*

If you have discovered a deer, and are in a stalking situation, you need to pick up your foot with your toes pointed downward to keep your boot tip from catching on any vines or brush. When you bring your foot down keep your toes pointed downward to get through any brush or noisy vegetation. Then straighten your foot out as it nears the ground, landing on the ball of your foot and then put more and more of your body weight in contact with the earth as the rest of your foot flattens out. All this time you should be feeling with your toes for any brittle twigs or branches. If you want to see this same motion in nature, watch a cat stalking a bird or an alerted doe or buck as it minces its way across a dry leaf covered forest floor.

Move only when the deer's head is down or facing directly away from you. Take a few quick quiet steps and stop with your human form screened by vegetation and wait for the animal to lift or turn its head. Wait until it lowers its head again or looks away and then repeat your previous performance. If you have little cover, move in a crouched position and rest with one knee on the ground. Watch the deer's mouth and body language, if he stops chewing, seems to tense up slightly, jerks his head up, funnels his ears in your direction or his body seems to stiffen, these are all signals that he senses that something is wrong. He's not sure what it is yet but his senses are on "red alert."

As you cautiously glide through the woods, pre-plan your approach for the least amount of noise and body movement and the most amount of cover. Establish a mental picture of your proposed path which your feet can follow without further visual confirmation. By pre-planning in this manner, you can walk a few steps without having to look down, which greatly increases your visual perspective and awareness. *Use a peek and sneak approach. Every few steps will open up new possibilities, which should be carefully analyzed before moving on.* Analyze the habitat with your eyes and then with your binoculars. Carefully inspect brush enveloped locations and dark recesses where your normal vision will not take you. Take advantage of, and examine any openings or sight lanes into potential cover. If possible, move with the sun at your back, but this is not more important than following the normal traffic flow and the appropriate wind orientation.

If you feel that you have located an interesting spot, don't be afraid to sit or stand motionless for five, ten, fifteen minutes or a half hour or more. The "grass is always greener" mentality has saved a lot of wide antlered bucks.

When you spot a deer, never move when the deer's head is up, unless it is looking in the opposite direction. Deer have a very broad range of peripheral vision. Even when a deer's head is turned at a slightly different angle or its head is down while feeding, it can see several yards in every direction.

A deer is nervous when it's feeding, because it knows that its hearing and sight are limited and will pop its head up every few seconds to check out the scenery. If it is alerted, not only will it rotate its eyes upward while feeding, but it will also pretend to put its head down to feed and then immediately pop it back up again. If undisturbed, while feeding, a deer will sometimes flick its tail just before bringing its head back up.

SEEING IS BELIEVING:

A good part of "seeing", is knowing how, where, and what to look for. To hunt successfully, we must learn how to distinguish and identify specific forms in the woods. *Look for detail not just the overall picture.* As in a jig-saw puzzle, if you look for bits and pieces, you'll find the whole, but if you look for the whole, you'll get nowhere. Train your eyes to look into and through vegetation, rather than around it. This is where a good set of binoculars makes a world of difference! *Try to see how much you can see in the landscape rather than how much landscape you can see!*

Learning how and what to look for can be taught. Learning where to look comes only with experience. *Train your eyes and mind to search for and analyze details!* You can practice visual awareness during your daily routines by searching out details in your every day environment.

When you are searching the terrain you should move your eyes first and then slowly rotate your head in a sweeping motion to pick out any "obvious" animals. Then dissect the cover in visual segments. Search out the most promising areas and the closest areas first, then those less promising areas, and then the areas further away.

Look first for movement, since movement is what first alerts us to an animals presence in heavy cover. Analyze the source of any and all movement, especially on otherwise calm days. Then concentrate on shape, color, and texture. If you don't know what your quarry looks like in its natural environment, look for photos which will teach you. Post cards and calendars do not make good study material. Look for photos of deer showing what they look like in real life hunting situations.

Remember that it takes little to no cover to hide a motionless deer. Practice the use of your peripheral vision since this part of a human's eye detects movement better than our forward vision. Vitamin A can also help us in having better night vision for those critical dawn and dusk hours.

Little things can pay big dividends! Concentrate on animal shapes and colors and look for bits and pieces, such as a cone-shaped ear, a cylindrical nose or the graceful curve of a leg. Remember that a deer's leg gets bigger as it moves up while a tree trunk gets smaller. Realize that a mature deer stands only 40 to 45 inches high at the shoulder and adjust your line of sight accordingly. The horizontal lines of a deer's back is easily identifiable in contrast to the vertical orientation of trees in a dense stand of fir trees. I have located numerous deer by this technique. In brush thickets look for solid forms which do not fit into the pattern of light and dark.

Analyze colors such as the white or gray color of an old buck's nose, the white around a mature buck's eyes, a white throat patch, or the current color of a buck's hide which will be a light, reddish tan in early August and September and a dark brown in the fall.

Note the white around the eyes and nose which help locate this buck.

The white throat patch and grey nose help identify this buck.

Good use of natural cover.

Look in locations which you feel might hold a nice buck. Look for any slight motion (the twitching of an ear or tail, as the deer tries to rid itself of a pesky fly), the glint of sunlight off a wet antler, or unusual color variations. I once saw a nice buck out in the center of a clear cut, because of the white flash caused when he lifted his leg to urinate on himself during the rut. Another time I detected a buck because his whitish grey nose contrasted with the dark, shaded, boulder-strewn hill on which he stood. I have located deer by using all of the above examples.

Don't move until you feel that you have carefully analyzed all available cover within your range of sight and then do a quick overview of all the areas again before you move on. Don't forget to check the areas to either side of you and also behind you. Many times deer will let you walk past them and then will sneak out behind you. I remember an old buck who let me walk past his hideout and then broke cover after I had taken three or four steps into a dense thicket of fir trees. I heard him break cover but by the time I had extracted myself from the thicket, he was disappearing over a nearby ridge, his tail waving me good-bye!

Purchase the best pair of 7 x 50 binoculars you can afford and use them to delve deep into the tangles of branches, probing into and through dark shaded areas, and generally dissecting your area of vision with your magnified sight. Focus on the inside of the brush, rather than on the periphery, so that you can look into the choicest locations. You'll be amazed at what you see. I will devote an entire chapter to the selection and purchase of optics.

Don't do all of your looking standing up at eye level. Get down to the deer's level and check out the landscape from their perspective. If you're a still hunter and don't wear out the knees of your hunting pants in one or two hunting seasons, then you're standing too much. This technique will open up a whole new visual dimension to your inquisitive eyes.

When you do locate a deer, analyze its shape, form and color, then determine what it was that caught your attention. Was it sight or sound? If it was sight, was it movement or was it form? Then paint a mental picture in your brain so that when you see a similar set-up in the woods, your recognition and response will come automatically. Many times I have located deer in the woods by instinct without being able to determine what first prompted my further investigation.

Remember that a buck's body color is generally darker than a doe's or an immature buck. A buck will walk more cautiously than a doe and will generally do a better job of screening his form. He will be the last to enter an opening, the first to leave, and will normally stay on the fringes rather than expose himself needlessly. An undisturbed buck, even if it's a small buck will walk differently than a doe, with his head held high and proud. With practice you can learn to tell whether a deer is a buck or a doe just by these visual characteristics, even before you see antlers. Remember the type of habitat in which you found the deer, the location of the deer in that habitat, the time of day and the weather and wind characteristics. The best detective work is done by asking questions. Was he feeding, bedded, traveling between areas, or spooked? Was he traveling on a well-used deer trail? Why do you think he was there? Where did he come from and where was he going? Was he in a fringe area where heavy brush blends into more open areas? Was he bedded in heavy timber or on the edge of a small ridge, etc. etc.?

Many hunters look at deer in their natural habitat but never "see" them, or if they do happen to stumble onto a deer they do not try to analyze why the deer was there. *Their senses have not been trained to react or to register what they see in a meaningful manner. Every shape or form in the woods has meaning to the person who studies it. Everything is intertwined into a network of cause and effect.*

Once you have discovered what types of habitat the deer prefer, what geographical characteristics control or direct their travel patterns, and how various weather and wind conditions affect deer movement you can use this information in new locations to make your time spent in the woods more effective and enjoyable. Successful still hunting is not for daydreamers or those who take their hunting casually. The deer have all the advantages. All we have is our intellect and a few skills which we should always be trying to perfect.

In still hunting, as in the life of a big old buck, the slow cautious one wins!!

Chapter 9

Out on a Limb
Effective Tree Stand Techniques

I am a still hunter at heart and like nothing better than to creep through the woods trying to outsmart a wary old buck, but since I turned to hunting for large antlered bucks, I rely almost exclusively on tree stands, either natural or manmade. When I first started using tree stands you couldn't even buy a stand in Oregon and about the only stand in the catalogues was the Baker Tree Stand. Since this time there have been numerous additions to the tree stand family and many improvements in design, portability and weight. Over the years I have learned a lot, had a lot of fun and made my share of mistakes, but I have also had enough successes that I know what it takes to make tree stands successful.

The reasons for the use of tree stands are numerous. 1. A hunter can watch instead of being watched. 2. Using a tree stand gives a trophy hunter time to study the deer and analyze antler size before deciding to shoot. In still hunting a hunter usually has only a split second to decide whether or not to shoot, and this is inadequate time to carefully analyze antler size. All bucks look big when they're running through the woods. 3. By being up in the air a hunter can better control his or her scent (yes, there are very good women hunters and yes, they do smell, too) and sound and hide any stray movements which may alert a cautious buck. 4. By being elevated you have better visibility in the brush-choked habitat typical of the country I hunt. A tree stand allows you to look into, rather than trying to look through, vegetation. 5. Being in a tree stand allows shots at undisturbed game, usually at close range and assures a quick clean kill. A hunter owes this much to the game he or she pursues. 6. Tree stands allow the hunter to effectively hunt the first few minutes of legal shooting light in the morning and the last few minutes in the evening. 7. Tree stands allow a hunter to take advantage of the fact that deer normally do not look up for danger. But this does not mean that you can make unnecessary movement or fail to screen your hunter form while you are in your stand. 8. Given the carelessness of other hunters, tree stands are a safe way to hunt. At least all you have to worry about is your own carelessness. It's pretty hard for another hunter to take a "brush shot" at a motionless hunter up in a tree. 9. The use of a properly placed tree stand and the use of the appropriate scent containment procedures allows you to hunt an area on a continuing basis without spooking the

Photo credit: Chuck Bartlett

Watching undisturbed bucks at close distances is what tree stands are all about!

deer and making them more cautious. 10. Last but definitely not least, I hunt from tree stands for the pure joy of watching undisturbed deer and game animals doing what they do naturally. This has allowed me to have many enjoyable hours and learn much about deer behavior.

The following are rules and guidelines to follow in setting up and using tree stands. Sure, you can break some of these rules and still be successful. But if you desire to consistently shoot large bucks you'd better not break them too often! This section is written in a point-by-point discussion to conserve space. An entire book could easily be written on tree stand hunting. This chapter is meant to be more informative than entertaining. Hopefully this information will allow you to accomplish your own entertainment.

1. Always use a safety belt while sitting in your stand and always check your steps before putting your full weight on them. I've taken a couple of pretty good spills by ignoring this rule.

2. Never set up a tree stand without analyzing the trails you intend to watch for a least 100 to 300 yards in either direction, to determine the common activity patterns and direction of travel. I went to a lot of work once setting up a stand which I believed would be excellent. (For that matter I have set up a fair number of stands which did not produce as I expected. But my percentage gets better every year.) Anyway, this stand was set up to watch what I thought was a primary feeding spot. Several trails meandered through a thick brush-choked hillside to reach my chosen point of interception.

During my evening vigils I saw a few deer, but never as many as I expected. Finally, I got smart and did what I should have done in the first place, and back tracked the trails which led toward my stand. By doing this I found out that this was really a secondary feeding location. The primary location was another 100 yards closer to the preferred bedding area. Deer were feeding near my stand location but they were using it predominantly after dark.

Needless to say, I immediately moved my stand. But I would have saved a lot of needless work and several unsuccessful nights if I had analyzed the trails more completely the first time.

Analyze where the deer are coming from, why they are using the trail or trails, and when the trails are being used. Setting up a tree stand is a lot of work, and a lot of wasted effort and unnatural commotion can be saved by careful analysis of the situation. *Don't be in a hurry to set up a stand at the first indication of animal activity. Slow down and think it through!!*

3. Study wind directions under varying weather situations. If you are unable to do this, know at the least, the typical wind direction and pattern of animal movement during the time of the day you intend to hunt. If the wind direction changes and is contrary to what is typical, leave immediately!! *Never use a tree stand under incorrect wind directions or gusty and varying wind directions.* If you do, you are only alerting the deer to your presence and lessening your chances of success, not only on this particular day, but also in the future. Weather, which creates a steady, mild, predictable wind pattern, will produce the most consistent results.

4. *A preplanned approach to your stand is critical for scent concealment (on trails and wind related), visual concealment and sound concealment. Never travel on or across any trail which you are planning to watch or through an area you intend to hunt. When you leave your stand, also try not to alert or alarm the animals you're hunting.*

5. Don't be afraid to experiment. Use several tree stand locations to take advantage of the various wind and weather conditions, movement patterns at various times of the day and season, and differing types of habitat. The deer change their travel and behavior patterns and you should be prepared for these changes.

6. Never betray your stand location to other game animals or for that matter other hunters. A tree stand is a very private hunting situation and except for the case of a stand situated on an escape route, additional human involvement will only weaken your chance of success. Further betrayal of your position to other wildlife may cause the deer to change their travel corridors and avoid the area you hunt all together.

7. If you are interested in trophy bucks never set up a tree stand out in the open, and don't waste your time placing

Photo credit: Chuck Bartlett

Position yourself near this guys travel route, with the correct wind orientation and scent control and you've got him!

your stand overlooking large, totally open spaces. Trophy bucks need cover before they feel safe entering a particular area. Sure, you may see tracks in these open spaces but this activity typically occurs long after legal shooting time.

8. *If possible, prepare your stand several months prior to the time you intend to hunt and do not enter the area again until hunting season begins.* If you cut branches, or clear brush for visibility, or to open up shooting lanes, remove all signs of activity. Darken the ends of the freshly cut branches or trees with dirt or cover them with moss or some other natural cover. Never remove any more vegetation than you absolutely have too!! Deer notice even small changes in their "living room", just as we would if someone came in and rearranged the furniture in our home.

If you are bow hunting, test fire a few shots to make sure there are no obstructions in your shooting lane. If you're a rifle hunter bring your rifle to a firing position to see if you can do so quietly and inconspicuously. Also, check out your potential deer viewing locations to make sure that there is no vegetation which would obstruct your vision or cause bullet or arrow deflection.

Portable stands can be used on the spur of the moment to produce success. I have taken a couple of nice bucks in this manner, but it is better to pre-scout and set up your stands long before you intend to hunt.

9. *If you plan to use a particular stand on a continuing basis you must practice all of the scent concealment and containment techniques covered in the chapter on scents, to be consistently successful.* Wear rubber or scent camouflaged gloves when climbing into your stand. Do not touch items on or around your stand with your bare hands and do not part branches with your bare hands while approaching your stand. In fact, keep your body contact with vegetation at a minimum for at least 100 yards before you reach your special spot.

Photo credit: Chuck Bartlett

If you want to catch a big mature buck like this you have to be very careful with scent contamination.

Remember that the longer you stay in a stand, the better the chance a deer has to pick up your scent and the more residual scent you leave at your location. Only stay as long as you need to! Scent has an oozing effect and will, unless there is a strong prevailing wind, gradually spread out and around a stationary hunter. This is especially true in foggy or misty weather, because of the low humidity.

10. *For an evening or morning stand you need to be prepared about a half hour to forty-five minutes before you expect the deer to arrive.* The reason for arriving several minutes early is so that the wildlife around your stand will have time to settle down and get back to their natural flow of movement and

sound. Then when the deer start to arrive the lack of natural animal sound and movement will not alert them to your location.

You should leave your stand as soon as you feel your chances of seeing a deer have ended. Leave as quietly and inconspicuously as possible, and again, be careful not to spread your scent or sound around and do not walk on any trails which you expect the deer to use during their evening travels. *You're leaving, but remember that a deer's evening has just begun!*

11. Do not scent-pollute your area. If you do, you may see does and small bucks, but the chances of collecting a really large buck are zero to none. *Remember that deer feed and travel all night long and they can smell and will react to your scent long after you are gone. Your physical body may be gone but your odor remains!!!*

12. The best stands are the ones from which you are able to watch several trails at the same time or watch the culmination of multiple trails. Morning trails, leading from feeding to bedding locations, go from specific to general and become less distinct as they approach potential bedding positions. Evening trails, leading to feeding locations on the other hand, go from the general (various bedding locations) to the specific. Again remember that blacktails do not have to travel far between bedding and primary feeding locations and that they will continue to browse and move all night long.

I am impatient, so I prefer evening stands, because the suspense continues to mount and your chances of seeing a trophy buck get better and better, the closer it gets to dark. In contrast, on a morning stand, given undisturbed animal movement patterns, the longer you are situated the less your chances are of seeing game. Also evening stands work better because you are watching a feeding location or are near a feeding location and you're able to observe the culmination of several trails at the same time.

As I mentioned earlier, in morning stands, which should be positioned between feeding and bedding locations, the trails tend to disperse rather than concentrate. You should try to place your morning stand 100 or more yards away from the general bedding locations or at natural funnels or geographical characteristics which concentrate travel lanes, so you can intercept as many deer as possible before they choose their specific indistinct path to their preferred hide-out.

Use the natural lay of the land to your advantage in constricting travel and thus increasing your potential of deer sightings. Hunting is a numbers game, and the more trails you can watch, all things being equal, the more deer you will see.

13. *Never wear the same clothes, while sitting on your tree stand, that you use to walk into the woods and always use the natural scent disguises and scent elimination procedures I talk about in the chapter on scents.*

14. *Never position your stand directly on the trail you are watching.* Always get off to one side or the other, depending on wind patterns and the deer's anticipated direction of travel.

15. Learn how to sit still. Try to avoid the "bob and weave syndrome" when you sense or hear an approaching animal. Assume that you are unnoticed and let the animal make the first move. Get comfortable and then don't move!!!

Set up your stand so that you can cover the most critical locations by simply moving your eyes. Nothing spooks a deer faster or catches his attention quicker than sudden movement. Visualize how fast even we as humans are alerted by such motion. The faster the motion the quicker our eyes are drawn to it.

Don't attempt to see everything around you. Visually concentrate instead on the habitat which you feel will produce the best chance of seeing a buck. *Let your ears do your looking for you and depend on them to alert you to the presence of game animals in the non-visual locations.* If you do hear a noise, don't want to wait, and you can't cover the area by simply moving your eyes, *slowly* turn your head until you can see what you need to see. But do so very, very slowly!!!

Once you have established your visual area of concern, position everything you need conveniently in front of you, so that everything can be reached with the least amount of movement and noise. Check for any branches, dried leaves or any other objects around you or on your presence which might create noise.

I have had bucks spook, or at least become alert, at the mere rubbing together of the rubber covers on my binoculars, the slight scraping of my wool shirt against rough tree bark and similar occurrences. I even set my watch on a nail or twig at eye level so I can tell what time it is when the deer show up. Everything I need is easily accessible with the least amount of movement on my part.

16. Don't be obvious. *Use natural camouflage as much as possible in front of, and especially, in back of you.* No form in the woods is so obvious as the form of a sky-lighted hunter. Use a three foot by eight foot piece of camouflage cloth with ties on the end to drape over your body or better yet tie it in front of you to break up your outline and also help cover possible movement. If possible, place your back up against a tree. This helps to give your back a rest, as well as breaking up your outline.

Wear face camo or a face mask and gloves to cover your shiny face and hands. If you use a face net cut out areas for your eyes and also for your ears. We cannot afford to limit our already weak senses in any manner. If you do have damaged or poor hearing there are several new hearing devices on the market to help you out.

Don't forget to camouflage your tree stand. Surprisingly some of the best tree stands still come with glossy paint or shiny unpainted metal. Use flat spray paints and cover all areas of the stand in contrasting colors. Do this a least two months or more, before the season starts, so that the paint odor will be long gone by the time you use it. It's also a good idea to actually leave the stand in the woods for a couple of weeks to further camouflage scent. You can set the stand in place or leave it at a handy location in the woods.

17. Once you are comfortably positioned, don't make any sounds!! No coughing, rustling of equipment, moving of feet, scraping of clothing against tree bark, sniffling, chewing gum, or similar actions. Never eat from or near your stand. This creates noise, odor and motion. Never go

Photo credit: Chuck Bartlett

You'll have to do better with your camouflage if you want to fool this guy!

to the bathroom from or near your stand. Yes, I know some people say that human urine will attract bucks. But this is the exception, rather than the rule, and only has a slight chance of happening during the height of the rut. Better safe than sorry! Remember we're playing the odds. Let's not lessen our already slim chances.

18. Stand hunting after a period of heavy rain can be very successful if the wind has settled down since deer become very active once the skies clear.

19. When you use a flashlight walking into your morning stand or coming out in the evening, it's a good idea to cover the light with red cellophane when you're within 300 to 400 yards or your stand. Also, if you are in unfamiliar country, mark your trail with surveyor's ribbon. Be sure and remove the ribbon when you're done. P.S. Always carry extra batteries, and duct tape the switch in the off position or place one battery in backwards so the flashlight won't accidently turn on while you're carrying it. It's no fun and can be potentially dangerous, trying to get out of the woods in the dark even if you know the area. I know, I've been there!

20. The average height of the stand should be 12 to 14 feet. But each situation is different, so you have to adjust your strategy to fit the situation. I've shot bucks from natural tree stands which were only four or five feet tall and I've positioned stands that were 20 or more feet high.

21. *Be prepared at all times! Never* let your guard down!!!!!

Have faith in your location, at least until it proves otherwise or the wind and weather changes. *Remember that it takes only one deer to end your season and it only takes a few seconds for that deer to show!* Deer, especially large bucks, have the annoying habit of suddenly materializing out of nowhere. One second nothing, the next the trophy of a lifetime. *To he or she who is alert and ready the prize awaits!*

I got so used to watching deer, at one of my tree stand locations, that I actually watched a Boone and Crockett 4 x 4 walk past my stand, at about 40 yards, without shooting.

When he entered my area I had picked up my binoculars, as I always do, to get a close up look before shooting, but instead of entering into the feeding area, he simply cut across one corner of it and melted back into the forest. By the time I realized what he was doing it was too late to reach for my rifle. I never saw him again.

22. Concentrate on looking and analyzing. Do not dwell on the cold, itches, stiff legs, sore seat or any of the multitude of items we as hunters tend to spend our time worrying about. Anticipate these tendencies and correct them when you first arrive. Accentuate the positive and don't dwell on the negative!!!

23. If it's cold always over-dress for warmth. Wear more clothes than you need and put them on before you start to get cold. When you're sitting motionless for long periods of time your body does not generate adequate heat to keep you comfortable without the aid of additional insulators. *Protect the most critical heat loss locations in this order of significance: your head, feet, hands and seat.* Wear a warm wool, polar-tec or insulated hat, neck warmer, warm socks and boots, and warm gloves and sit on a thin insulated seat pad to protect yourself from moisture and ground chill. I always carry a couple of disposable hand and foot warmers which I use on very cold days. A thin pair of disposable plastic gloves worn under your outer gloves works great in cold, wet, windy weather.

Being cold creates a cycle. The cold penetrates your body, which causes you to be uncomfortable, which causes unnecessary discomfort and movement, which spells failure. If you have done all that you can and still feel like you're starting to get cold, do isometric exercises to get your blood circulating again.

24. If you're one of those people who absolutely cannot sit still for more than 15 minutes to half an hour, you can still be a successful stand hunter. Simply plan your route through the woods so you can still hunt to predetermined spots and stop for as long as you can at each location. Again, to be successful, you need to know the regular animal movement patterns in relation to the prevailing wind direction.

25. Be aware of a deer's peripheral vision. Even when you're up a tree move only when the deer's head is down, and preferably when he is looking in the opposite direction.

26. In brush-filled terrain, if you know where the bedding and potential feeding locations are, you might try making your own travel lanes through the woods by clearing out brush and making one or more trails between these areas. You can even construct turns or obstructions which cause the deer to pause where you have good visibility or a chance for a shot. Again, do this several months before the season and place your stand off to one side, located with wind direction and anticipated direction of travel in mind.

27. Stands do not need to be artificial. You can find many good, natural stands in the woods which you can use to your advantage. I've shot several bucks while using natural stands. I shot one very nice four point while perched on top of a natural tree stand, formed when a falling fir tree lodged in the crotch of an old maple tree. I shot another buck while sitting on top of an old pile of logs and I outsmarted a large, old three point once by simply using an old rotted stump as a back rest, and placing maple leaves and moss over the front of my body to screen my outline. This buck looked directly at me from 20 to 30 yards, with no sign of fear or recognition. After watching him for several minutes, I shot him in the neck when he put his head down to feed.

28. *Don't let the prime determination of where you position your stand be based on how much area you can cover visually. It's not how much or how far you see, but rather, the quality of what you see that's important.* I've seen hunters watch sterile, cut over areas and open meadows for hours on end with no success, except the possible occasional glimpse of a doe or small buck. Blacktail deer are not like mule deer; they do not need long areas of visibility to be secure. *Their security is established by the strategic use of any and all cover available to them.*

29. Don't forget the mid-day stand locations to cover the activity pattern between 10:00 and 12:00. Read the chapter

Photo credit: Boyd Iverson

It's hard to tell buck from branches!

entitled "Moon Madness". During these mid-day activity patterns, deer will get up from their beds, stretch and check out the surrounding terrain, go to the bathroom, possibly grab a few bites to eat and then bed down again, taking into consideration any changes in sun location and wind direction. On hot days, deer will try to remain in the shade, and on cold days, they will try to pick up any stray heat rays. These stands should be located on the periphery of suspected bedding locations and security cover and on trails between these two locations. Again, the stand should be placed with the prevailing wind or thermals in mind.

30. The most successful, and in my mind, the most fun stands, are the ones which are set up in undisturbed locations so that you can predetermine the natural pattern of deer movement and install your stand to cover this anticipated movement.

31. However, tree stands strategically located so that they are able to watch escape trails and trails which funnel deer activity, can also be very successful, if you hunt in an area where there is a lot of other hunter activity. Here, your stand is positioned to take advantage of the inability of other hunters to sit still.

Escape trails will be the ones which show the most sign of the running deer. They will usually be positioned near bedding areas, lead to heavy cover, and will usually travel sidehill or downhill.

There is one trail in an area where I hunt, coming off the tip of a steep finger ridge, which never has any tracks on it until there is heavy hunting pressure. Above this escape trail is a small but thick stand of fir trees. In this stand of fir trees is the heaviest concentration of deer beds I have ever seen. The bucks bed in this thicket with visibility in either direction, and escape down this and another trail leading down the other side of the ridge when hunters approach.

Photo credit: Chuck Bartlett

In a dim light situation you need to grab all the light you can.

These escape trails will generally not be long, maybe 50 to 150 yards. Smart deer do not run very fast, very far. B.J. Schurtleff, a bow hunter, shot a blacktail buck which used to be the all-around world record by watching an escape trail.

32. Do not position your stand right at a feeding location in the morning, or a bedding location in the evening. Pick a mid-way point.

33. Position your stand where you will have the greatest amount of shooting light. Large bucks leave feeding locations at, or before, daylight in the morning and arrive at feeding locations just prior to or after dark in the evening. Your best chance for a shot is to position your

stand nearer the bedding areas in morning, at small, secluded feeding locations in the evening or a few hundred yards away from the larger more exposed feeding locations in the evening. But be sure and place your stand in a location which lets in as much light as possible when you are back in the woods and away from the openings.

If you are in a deep woods situation, which blocks out most of the available sunlight, you would have a better chance of success by placing your stand at, or near, the anticipated opening where you expect them to feed. Even though the deer will be arriving later, your hunting time will be extended, since there is more available light in this more open environment. *Also, on your evening stands, pay very careful attention to the sun setting and moon rising tables to take advantage of all available light.* For a more in depth discussion of this concept, see the chapter entitled "Moon Madness".

34. Purchase the best light gathering scope and binoculars you can afford. A friend of mine was not able to shoot at a buck which he spotted with his naked eye because of the poor quality of the optics which he had mounted on his rifle. There is an old tried and true saying which is appropriate, "You can't shoot it if you can't see it."

Do not hunt with open sights even in rainy situations (which is most of the time in Oregon). You will only be unnecessarily hindering your chances of success. I will talk more about specific binocular and scope choices in the chapter on optics.

35. It's a good idea to carry a few small rocks, and or sling shot, into your tree stand. Use them to try and direct a buck's travel in your direction by creating a disturbance on the far side of him. I've even used rocks to get deer to leave my stand location after dark so that they will not be alerted to my presence. I have been "trapped" several times

by deer which bedded down or continued to feed within a few yards of my stand long after dusk.

36. If you are bow hunting, predetermine the distances to familiar objects around so you that when a deer shows you do not have to guess at the distance. Also, take practice shots at these distances, prior to the season, so that you will know exactly where to aim. If you believe in the use of scents you might even take practice arrows and add a masking scent or attracting scent and fire the arrows to different spots around your stand.

I have heard some hunters say that stand hunting is no fun and is just a matter of luck and being in the right spot at the right time.

But these hunters have not taken the time to learn the art of stand hunting. *Consistent successful stand hunting is a lot of fun and any "luck" you have is created by your knowledge of deer behavior, of weather and wind variables, and the travel patterns of the animals in the habitat where you choose to hunt.* As I've said before, it takes a lot of work and knowledge to be consistently "lucky".

If you feel like there is a heck of a lot of information to learn and that I sound like a fanatic in my hunting practices, you're right on both counts. There are a multitude of variables which affect the success of every hunting situation and it only takes "one little" mistake or oversight to cost you a trophy buck. *The more attention you pay to detail and the more observations you make, and notes you take, the better.* You cannot be too careful or do too much analyzing.

Because of what I have been able to learn about wildlife habits while tree stand hunting, I have had several large bucks literally walk under, stand under, and feed directly beneath my stand. I've had large bucks so close I could hear the sound of grass tearing as they pulled it out of the ground while feeding. I've heard them chew, heard their

Photo credit: Chuck Bartlett

These are the up close and personal situations which make hunting from tree stands so much fun!

stomachs grumble, and heard their pellets hit the ground when they went to the bathroom.

I have had the fun of witnessing several sparring matches, watched bucks chase estrous does within a few feet of me, had bucks walk completely around my stand, observed numerous black bear and coyotes travel by within a few yards, and had up to 14 deer around me at one time. I've seen eleven bucks in one evening (several of which were large mature bucks) and had bucks bed down within a few yards of me and literally "trap" me in my stand until several hours after dark. If this doesn't sound like fun then I don't know what is!

Since I started hunting, my longest shots taken from a stand have been between 35 to 40 steps, and my closest, six steps. Several of the 35 to 40 yard shots could have been closer but I couldn't stand the tension any longer, so I fired. Plus a couple of the shots would have been even closer than six steps, however I was afraid that my movement would spook the bucks so I let them pass and took my shot when they were further away.

Stand hunting is a lot of fun and gives you some fantastic opportunities to watch big game animals and other wildlife, in their natural, undisturbed habitat. If you decide to follow the techniques covered in this book, as well as additional techniques which you will discover on your own, you will have the opportunity to enjoy the same sort of experiences yourself.

HUNTERS, TAKE YOUR STAND!!

Chapter 10

Scents and Nonsense

The Use and Misuse of Scents

This chapter analyzes a deer's sense of smell as it relates to our hunting success. We will cover such questions as: How far away can animals smell us? What is scent? How does a deer smell us? How can we protect ourselves from a deer's nose? How do we use scents to our advantage? Where are a deer's scent glands located and how are they used?

A deer's sense of smell is its only independent and immediate tip off to our, or any other predator's presence. Eyes and ears can be fooled to the point where an animal needs other sensual affirmation; *but if a deer gets a nose full of human scent the game's over!* For this reason our first concern should be in limiting our "scent pollution". *Remember also, that your human odor remains long after your physical body has left, and that this odor continues to have an adverse affect on all animals who discover it.*

A deer's ability to receive and distinguish scent is dependent on two things; the amount of molecules of a particular odor, and the amount of moisture or humidity in the air. Odors are made up of invisible molecules of gas which must be mixed with moisture to be recognizable. The more humid the air the more easily scents are picked up and identified. That is why the noses of game animals are always moist and why deer lick their noses in dry weather. This is also why bucks, during the rut, are continually licking their noses, to help them pick up any lingering doe scent.

As a deer breathes, the gas molecules are inhaled and the different odor causing molecules come in contact with moisture in the deer's nose. This in turn stimulates the nerve endings, which then sends the information to the brain.

Other organs in a deer's nasal cavity help them distinguish the distinctive odor of other deer in the area. It is also believed that a deer and predators can tell the health and age of other deer by the smell emitted from urine or feces. This may be how predators are able to tell whether a particular animal is more vulnerable to attack.

Scientists believe that humans have approximately 10 million olfactory receptors (more or less), while big game animals have several hundred million. In any case, a deer's sense of smell, even with a bad cold, is far superior to ours.

Game animals are able to distinguish, sort through, and categorize several odors at the same time. This is why masking scents, such as skunk or fox urine alone, are not sufficient to block out uncared for human scent, or scents associated with human activity.

Game animals "label" odors as to whether they are natural or unnatural. The unnatural categories can elicit alarm, fear or merely curiosity. Natural scents elicit no response, fear, or in the case of sexual and territorial scents, attraction or caution.

It takes only a few drops of human perspiration for an animal to detect us, even at distances of up to 200 to 300 yards. With the amount of human scent contamination which many hunters carry into the woods, it's amazing that they don't put every deer in the country into flight or hiding! But then again, maybe they do!!

Biologists believe that a dog's senses are very similar to that of big game animals, and in scientifically controlled studies, dogs showed owner recognition at 225 to 310 yards. Big game animals, tested under similar situations, showed scent recognition from 175 to 285 yards. Remember our previous statement about scent remaining long after we leave the area, and then consider the fact that bloodhounds can scent track people even when the trail is several days old. Now do you understand why limiting and disguising our human odor is so important?

One scent experimenter used a substance associated with human odor and then diluted it 1:100,000 with water. He then released one cubic centimeter of this mixture into the air at various temperature ranges. At a distance of 100 yards there was a reaction to the odor noted by 90% of the game animals tested. If you feel sweat on your face after physical exertion, the amount of moisture on your head would be twice what was used in the test noted above. The longer perspiration is allowed to remain on your body the more odor is produced, as odor is cumulative. If it gets to the point where even we can smell ourselves, it has definitely exceeded all levels of tolerance for an animals' senses.

A deer has four major scent glands; the tarsal, the metatarsal, the pre-orbital and the interdigital. The metatarsal gland is located on the outside of a deer's leg and secretes an alarm scent which has a garlic type odor. Since you are what you eat, you don't want to eat foods seasoned with garlic during the hunting season. Fir tree growers have even developed a chemical which smells like garlic, which they spray on their seedlings to help keep deer from destroying them.

The pre-orbital glands are located on the forehead next to the eyes. These glands are rubbed on branches to set up home range boundaries and may be used to show dominance among bucks. This is the scent gland that a buck rubs on the overhanging branches of trees as a scent post and also produces the scent which is left when a buck rubs his antlers on trees during the summer months to remove velvet or when he spars with trees in mock battle during the rut. I have seen large bucks rub this gland on overhanging branches near feeding areas both before and during the rut. I have never observed small bucks doing this, so this act must have something to do with dominance or hierarchy.

The interdigital scent is located in the thick hair between a deer's hooves. This gland leaves a scent, on the ground, as the deer walks and allows other deer to know who has traveled on the trail before them, and indicates the presence of any new deer in the neighborhood. A doe uses the scent trail, laid down by this gland, to track and identify her fawns and a fawn uses it to locate its mother when they are separated. This gland can be skinned out and frozen or otherwise preserved for future use in covering our human scent.

The last important scent gland is the tarsal gland which is located on the inside of the rear legs. This gland is used for recognition, for transmittal of sexual stimuli on bucks and does and is believed to indicate the age and the sex of an animal. It becomes dark red and discolored on a buck during the rut and a dark red to black color when a doe is in estrus. I've watched bucks urinate on these glands and then rub their legs together during the rut. This gland emits a very strong, pungent odor even after the buck has left the area. It may be used as a locator for estrous does, since I have seen does hang around specific core locations during the breeding season, waiting for a buck to show.

The locations which they choose to wait at are usually located between feeding and bedding locations, near major

Photo credit: Chuck Bartlett

Large buck rubbing his pre-orbital gland on a branch during the rut.

travel ways, or near prime feeding locations. Does will generally bed down right in the open, in the feeding location, near the major travel routes or at the intersections of major travel corridors.

HOW CAN WE AS HUNTERS PROTECT OURSELVES FROM A DEER'S NOSE?

1. The First Steps Are Elimation and Prevention of Unnatural Human Odors!!

A. ELIMINATION: Elimination of unnatural scent is actually fairly easy if you follow these steps.

Don't smoke, use after-shave or colognes, perfumed soaps, scented detergents, clothes softeners, scented chewing-gum or candy, hair sprays, scented deodorants, standard insect repellents and similar unnatural products. Use natural oils and cleaners on your guns and bows. Don't use silicone-based water repellant, snow sealers, or chemical water repellents on your boots, hats, or clothes. A company called Country Cover even makes a natural smelling gun oil, bore cleaner and lubricant, and another company called Montana Pitch Blend makes a pine-based water repellent leather dressing for boots. Several companies now make unscented laundry soap, and James Co. has a scent stopping boot cream you can use on your boots. You can even make your own unscented or natural scented soaps, or buy one of the many unscented soaps now on the market.

If possible, a hunter should have two complete sets of hunting clothes. Wear these clothes, hats and boots only for hunting and only in the woods when you're hunting. Do not wear them at work, home or around camp. For at least two weeks prior to the season and after each day's hunt, keep your clothes, boots and hunting pack stored in sealed

Photo credit: Chuck Bartlett

Large buck rubbing his tarsal glands together during the rut.

plastic bags intermixed with natural scent producing plants common to the area you intend to hunt. Wash each set of clothes after 1 to 2 days of use and put them back in their scent bag.

If you intend to stand hunt, wear different clothes walking into and away from the stand, than you use while hunting from your stand. Put your actual hunting clothes on within 100 to 200 yards of your stand location and when you leave, change back into your hiking clothes, a similar distance from your stand.

Since deer track other deer by the interdigital scent located between their hooves, and the tarsal scent located on the lower part of the deer's leg, they are particularly sensitive to unnatural scents on the boots and the lower pant legs of hunters. Wear rubber boots that have been exposed to natural smells for a prolonged period of time, since new rubber boots have a very distinctive odor, or wear leather boots and use one of the commercial scent eliminators in combination with natural scent camouflage. Rubber boots tend to sweat more than leather boots, so contrary to what is normally said, I prefer to use leather boots, with all of the appropriate scent containment practices.

As you are hunting, step in, rather than over, cow pies and deer droppings to help disguise foreign odors, and periodically rub natural scents into the sides and bottoms of your boots and the legs of your pants. You can also apply an interdigital scent to the bottoms and sides of your boots.

It is known that meat eaters and vegetarians emit different odors. In fact, I understand that the U.S. army had a sensing device which we used in Vietnam to distinguish between our troops, who were heavy meat eaters, and the Vietnamese who weren't. Indians used to purify their systems of all odors with steam baths and even refused to eat for a couple of days prior to the hunt. So it would make sense to have a vegetarian, pasta, bread, cheese and milk type diet for two to three weeks prior to deer season and to continue such a diet as long as the season lasted. As a further benefit, it has been shown that a carbohydrate diet supplies more energy for physical exercise than does a meat diet.

Some people believe that taking chlorophyll tablets gets rid of human scent. Since human odors are caused by bacterial action, not the scent itself, I'm not sure that this has any positive effect. But possibly, since chlorophyll is a green plant derivative, taking it for several days prior to the hunt may help in getting rid of or limiting our meat eating predator smell.

B) PREVENTION: Always wash your clothes with unscented or natural scented soaps, baking soda, or some of the new scent eliminating or neutralizing products. Before you enter the woods take a shower with unscented soap, and also use baking soda, or one of the other scent-elimination products on the market.

When you're in the woods, use natural masking scents you find in the area. Take periodic "baking soda baths" or reapplication of scent neutralizing products and local natural scent cover-ups. If you're a still-hunter, move slowly to limit perspiration. But also remember, that no matter how slow you move, your body normally emits one to two gallons of moisture, through perspiration, each day.

When still-hunting or when approaching my stand location, I take fir boughs, (noble firs have the strongest fragrance) crush them in my hands and vigorously rub them all over my body, and specifically on the sides and bottoms of my boots and lower pant legs. I then take the crushed needles and stuff them in my pockets for added scent protection.

In washing, and while hunting, pay special attention to your major scent locations, i.e., your head, hair, and forehead, in front of and behind your ears, underarms, back of the neck, lower back and chest.

Pay special attention to your extremities, your head, hands and feet. More heat is released through your head than any other part of your body, and in this case, heat equals perspiration, equals odor. We are also constantly touching vegetation with our hands while we are hunting. A sprinkling of baking soda, a scent elimination spray in your hair or a charcoal impregnated hat couldn't hurt.

Human hair is extremely smelly. That's why many people use human hair cuttings to keep deer out of their gardens.

Photo credit: Chuck Bartlett

If you're going to beat this guy's nose you're going to have to use all of the scent elimination techniques.

While stand hunting try using one of the throw away shower caps left in motel bathrooms, under your regular hunting hat, to contain odor from your head and also retain body heat in cold weather. Use fresh clean gloves and spray them with one of the scent elimination products. I would also recommend changing your hat and gloves or washing them after each day of hunting.

Furthermore, in case you haven't had the pleasure of smelling your socks or shoes lately, your feet stink! Change or wash your socks daily and use unscented antiperspirant on your feet. Your boots can also (with your wife's permission) be placed in the freezer for a few days to kill all odor-causing bacteria. But don't use baking soda inside your boots, for scent protection, as it can clog the interior liners which are supposed to breath. It is ok to spray the inside of your boots periodically with one of the liquid scent elimination products.

If you use a day pack or fanny pack, be sure and keep it scent free also.

The reason for the use of baking soda and some of the other scent elimination or prevention products, when bathing and while hunting, is that human odor is caused by bacterial action on the skin which attacks perspiration and creates odor. These products neutralize this bacterial action and actually keep odor from forming. Some of the new scent products out on the market today actually work on the molecular structure of odor and neutralize or eliminate it. I now use these neutralizing products along with baking soda.

There are also several clothing products out now, with scent elimination products built into them, and several companies have clothes with charcoal linings which will stop or contain human odor.

2. The Second Step Is Hiding or Disguising Human Odor.

There are many types of masking scents, but there are only two general varieties; natural animal scents and natural plant or earth scents. These scents are used to cover up or dilute human scent to such a degree that it is not easily or immediately distinguished by game animals. But as noted in the previous information about a deer's scenting ability and specifically its ability to sort through and distinguish several scents at the same time, *totally* disguising human odor is very hard or perhaps impossible to do. But we can at least delay the immediate identification of our smell or lessen the animal's reaction to our odor because of its dilution.

A. ANIMAL SCENTS: The most common animal disguising scents are skunk and fox. *Remember though, that a little goes a long way and that there may be no foxes or skunks in your area. If the scent is not common to the area you hunt do not use it, period!!!* If we think the product we're using is strong smelling, then multiply that thousands of times for the animal we're hunting. My belief is that too much of any animal scent is not wise and will alarm deer, or at the least, put them on the alert. Some hunters believe in using scent bombs around their stands to knock out human scent. I believe that this sells more scents than it fools deer. If we have taken the appropriate precautions with bathing, scent elimination sprays, natural cover scents, and wind direction, scent bombs are not needed.

On the other hand, B. G. Schurtlef, a very successful hunter and a man who has taken several large blacktail bucks, one of which is one of the largest blacktails ever taken with a bow, would argue strongly with me on this issue. He believes in using scent bombs made from skunk scent and specific doe-in-heat scents during the rutting period and places them strategically around his tree stand to control human odor and attract game. It obviously works for him. As in any hunting situation use what works for you. If you've had good experience and perfected the use of disguise and attractor scents, then use them.

The concept behind the use of smaller predator scents, such as fox, is to choose one common to your area. The belief is that when the deer smell this common odor, they feel safe.

My personal belief is that these types of scents do more potential harm than good! If used at all, these scents, and in fact all animal scents, should be used sparingly and with knowledge, and should not be put directly on your clothing. Use a scent vent, a cotton or wool swath pinned to your pants, boot pads, athletic wrist sweat-band wrapped around your boots, or strips of cotton rags dipped in scent and tied to shoe strings tied around your boots. *If you use any of these scents do not intermix them! Always use rubber gloves when handling scents so that you do not pollute the natural scent with your unnatural scent.*

If you are stand-hunting do not carry any of the animal scents to your stand. Leave them at strategic points near the area you are watching. If you have any string with you, you might want to place them 14" to 18" inches above the ground for better scent dispersal. Also if you're stand-hunting you can place the scent in cotton-filled, marked, 35 millimeter film canisters, with holes drilled in them or one of the heated scent dispensing wicks, at various locations around you, to help cover your human scent. I would suggest tossing the canister to areas where you want them to be. If you walk over to each spot you will be leaving a scent trail at each location, thereby doing more harm than good.

Be sure and pick up all of the containers when you leave.

B. PLANT SCENTS. The most common purchased plant scents are sage, pine and natural earth scent. Be sure to only use scents found in your area. Turpentine in areas with pine trees, acorn scent in areas with acorn trees, cedar oil or incense cedar strips in areas with cedar trees and so on. These scents should be spread over your entire body, but again pay special attention to your high sweat areas and direct contact areas such as pant legs and boots. Use more scent on high humidity days and less on low humidity days. You can create your own natural plant scents by boiling herbs or plants common to your area, straining out the remaining fiber from the concoction and putting this liquid in a bottle. Transfer this concentrate to a small spray atomizer, add rain water or an unscented alcohol and spray this on your clothes, footwear, hat and hair.

After several years of experimenting, I do not use skunk and fox type disguising scents and instead use scent elimination sprays and local, natural plant cover-up scents, exclusively. I periodically rub them vigorously over my entire body, my pant legs and the sides of my boots. I even grind them into the soles of my boots.

By using this technique I have had bucks cross my trail with no signs of recognition or alarm, put their noses to the trail I walked in on and even follow it for several feet with no alarm and stand down wind from me without immediately showing any signs of fear or recognition. I had one large, three point buck actually walk downwind of me after he detected my movement while I was still-hunting, and then approach to within 20 to 25 yards of where I was before deciding he had more important business elsewhere. I have had large bucks walk entirely around my tree stand, feed directly underneath me and even bed within a few yards of my location with no sign of alarm.

If you are going to experiment with scents, do it during the off season, or in areas other than your prime hunting area. *The key point with the use of all scents is to use them with knowledge and care and remember that a little goes a long way!*

ATTRACTING SCENTS AND SEX SCENTS

Attracting scents are made up of four major types; food, sex, curiosity and territorialism. Of these types, sex and territorial scents, if used properly, are the most effective. I do not believe that food attracting scents such as grape, apple, and acorn have any proven validity and certainly should not be used in an area where there are no such foods available. During the hunting season, food is in adequate supply and a small amount of scent dispensed from a bottle is not sufficient to draw in game.

The most common sex scents available are any of the common doe-in-heat products. I have had no proven success using such scents, but I do not generally hunt during the rut and my specific hunting techniques do not necessitate the use of such products. *If you do decide to use sex scents, make sure that they are 100% natural, are obtained only from deer and are fresh when you get them and fresh when you use them!*

I have experimented with sex scents and have had bucks walk directly over such scents with no response and have had a small doe come right up to a canister of scent, put her nose up to it and then jump back in fright. But my experience is certainly not all encompassing.

If you decide to use sex scents, never put them directly on your clothing. You do not want to direct a deer's eyes, ears and nose directly to your position. When you are not using the scents or the scent dispensers, keep them stored in plastic containers or bags and possibly keep them frozen. Read the manufacturers' directions. *Never use old scents!!*

Sex attracting scents should be used only during the rut, or better yet, just prior to the actual breeding dates. This is the really "hot time", when big bucks are most vulnerable, since it is the largest bucks who first react to the female challenge. *If you do not know the general breeding dates in your area, check with your local game biologist.*

The tarsal gland from previously killed deer can be used as an attractor scent as well as a means of disguising your human odor. If you use these glands be sure and freeze them as soon as possible and cut off pieces as you need them. Do not use scent glands from an estrous doe or buck killed during the rut except during similar hunting situations. Scent glands taken from deer killed during the rest of the season can be used anytime.

The scent glands you use do not have to be from deer killed in the same area. In fact a tarsal gland from a dominant buck from another area may be very effective in getting the attention of local bucks, who feel that a new buck has invaded their territory. These glands can be pinned to your pants below your knee with safety pins or can be tied to your boots with shoe strings and left to trail along the ground as you proceed through the woods. You can also put them in a bottle of alcohol and then put this solution in a small atomizer for future use. I've heard of one hunter who takes the tarsal gland from an estrous doe and ties it to his boots and then rubs it into every buck rub he passes, hoping that it will attract a dominant buck.

If you are using a tarsal gland and plan on still hunting all day and not heading to a stand location, be sure to continually check your back trail in hopes of catching a curious or territorially protective buck.

Deer urine can also be used as an attracting scent; the theory behind this being that the deer want to find out who the new boy on the block is. You can collect your own deer urine by carrying a small plastic bottle and syringe with you when you hunt. Put the bottle in the freezer as soon as you can after you have collected it. You can also

Photo credit: Chuck Bartlett

This buck is tracking a doe in heat.

mix it with Benzl Benzoate. If you do this it should keep without refrigeration. You can later mix it with rain water and put it in an atomizer for future use. Note: Be sure and tell your wife and children about your projects and label all of your containers!!

If you decide to use attracting scents and if you're planning on stand-hunting, use the same placement techniques we discussed for animal scents. Leave the scents at one or more strategic locations near the area you plan to watch and hang them 14" to 18" above the ground for better scent dispersal or use the film canister technique we talked about earlier.

Sex stimulants are generally close range attractors. If you use them in a stand situation, (in my belief this would be the best time to use them) you should *place the scents no more than 30 to 50 yards from your stand and in a location where the wind will blow the scent into nearby bedding areas or trails where you feel bucks will be traveling. Bucks can and do scent-check a breeding location from downwind, without having to expose themselves.* If they scent a doe they will proceed with their investigation.

One very successful hunter who has killed several large bucks, carefully hunts these scenting or viewing trails, which circle the small openings where the does prefer to feed during the breeding season.

Never use any scent that smells like garlic, as this is an alarm scent and will be avoided. You might consider using garlic or human hair clippings to "block off" trails which you aren't able to watch, in the hopes that the game will use your trail instead. You can even use it to cover escape trails which you and your hunting partners are not able to watch in a two man, still hunting situation.

A very important aspect to remember with scents, especially with sex scents and all the numerous products which

Photo credit: Chuck Bartlett

This buck is testing the air for any interesting female scent molecules.

are currently flooding the market, is that *scents can possibly help, if used correctly, but they are never the answer to instant success.* Sure, there are many instances of untrained hunters spraying a "sex attractant" all over their body and then having a big love-sick buck come up to them with its tongue hanging out of its mouth, asking them to shoot him. *But for each of these instances, I'm sure that there are hundreds of examples where the scent spooked, rather than attracted game!* Of course we and the scent manufacturers do not talk about these instances and in fact may not even be aware of them.

Don't try to substitute "scents for knowledge." There is no quick shot solution to consistently bagging big bucks. A hunter must do his homework and be continually alert and working to improve his knowledge of tactics and terrain. We need to learn the habits of deer in general, and the habits of the deer in our hunting area in particular.

I will promise you one thing though, and that is, that you can shoot large bucks by perfecting the techniques discussed in this book, without the need to use attracting scents to fill in the voids of your hunting knowledge.

I am not specifically speaking against the use of attracting scents, but I do feel that too much emphasis is being placed on them by the manufacturers and advertisers who profit by their sale. Thirty five years ago there were three or four scent manufacturers, now there must be forty or fifty, all claiming that their product is the best, and will cause big bucks to lose all caution and run madly in the direction of their product. *A lot of "cents" are made by companies selling "scents," so do your homework!*

If they worked as easily as all of the ads claim, there wouldn't be any big bucks left. Obviously there is more to it than that. *You can be sure that the people who have legitimate products, have many years of "woodsmanship" under their belts, and the use of scents is a by-product of an already extensive knowledge of deer and deer habits!* But you can also be sure that all of this information is not able to be contained on a product label or product literature.

I know of no legitimate scent manufacturer who started with the use of scents first. The use of scents was always a secondary step in their hunting education and came after many years of expertise and experimentation, to learn exactly how and when to use the product.

Just like any hunting "set-up", there are specific reasons and special situations and circumstances where varying techniques are successful. It takes a lot of research and hard work to learn what these circumstances are.

Attracting and sex scents can be more or less successful depending on weather conditions (wind and humidity specifically), temperature, time of year and time of day, method and amount of application, current movement patterns of deer in your hunting location, age and population mix of the animals you're hunting, and of course each animal's own unique personality. Scents should never be used as a cover-up for lack of knowledge or poor hunting ability, but rather as an addition to our bag of woods lore!

Chapter 11

Bits and Pieces

Information about Weather, The Rut, Rattling, Body Language, and other interesting hunting information

This section of the book will be devoted to short topics about what I, and other individuals, have observed about deer behavior. It is meant to provide various bits of useful information, which should make your time in the woods more enjoyable and successful.

BIG BUCKS ARE DIFFERENT:

Mature bucks like to feed in fringe areas and then find a secluded hillside to bed on during the day. *They generally do not use the major deer trails, but instead travel on the more indis-*

tinct side trails. During the rut these trails are cross wind or down wind of the major trails which are used heavily by does. They will bed within a few hundred yards of their initial evening feeding location though they may cover a mile or two in their night-time journeys. *Mature bucks will come out later in the evening and move into heavy bedding cover earlier in the morning than does and young bucks.* In a feeding situation they will monitor other deers' activity to see if everything is safe before exposing themselves. They do this, both visually, and through the use of their fine sense of smell. *Bucks will scent-check their trail and thereby know about every animal or human who has preceded them.* It is believed that they can even tell the sex and approximate age of other deer and can tell whether they were calm or alarmed as they proceed down the trail.

A buck will spend most of his lifetime in an area not much larger than one or two square miles, but a majority of his time is spent in an even more limited area called his core area. He will retreat to this area during periods of high hunting pressure or human disturbances. *The older the buck, the more restricted his movements will be during heavy hunting pressure and the more apt he is to stay in heavy cover, near preferred escape routes. Unless they are killed or the habitat is dramatically changed, large bucks will "always" return to their core area.*

Some interesting information was obtained by the Oregon Department of Fish and Game in 1997, during several evening photo sessions, with a camera attached to a motion detector.

These detectors were placed on several known trails which led from the high country down to lower country, on known migration routes.

It was discovered in this study that bucks typically traveled on *different trails* than the does and fawns. Also, surprisingly, 42% of the bucks photographed were four points

Photo credit: Chuck Bartlett

Happiness is a secure bed!

or better, while in the game departments typical evening spotlight counts during the winter months, 20% of the bucks were in this size category. This shows that even at night bucks are more secretive and do not associate with or spend time in the same areas as younger deer or deer of the opposite sex, except obviously during the rut.

Once a buck begins looking for does, normal travel patterns and actions are adjusted and it's a new game. Bucks move more all day long and typically more bucks are killed during this time than any other, but in actuality the activities of these bucks, during this time, is even less predictable than before. They show up in new areas and can do things which are down right stupid, in their search of the opposite sex.

When you take one large buck from an area, another buck will usually replace it by the following year! Also if you take good bucks from an area there will generally be other good bucks in the same location due to heredity and soil types.

When a group of deer are jumped, the buck will generally travel in a different direction than the rest of the deer. *Mature bucks will also use younger bucks and does as decoys and advance alarms.* This is not coincidence. How many times have you shot a smaller buck and then suddenly a larger buck materialized out of no-where. So don't spook any deer unless you want to ruin your chances for a larger buck. Exercise trigger control when you see smaller bucks; they could possibly be followed by "Mr. Big." *Larger bucks will even run with smaller bucks and use them as decoys during the rut.*

An older buck prefers to silently creep out ahead of a hunter or stay put, but will, as a last resort, if he feels that he's been discovered, break into a short, brush-busting run. Once there is protective cover between the hunter and the hunted, he reverts back to a slow cautious walk. The younger the deer, the further they will run when spooked.

In the evening, when coming into feeding locations, the does arrive first and then the smaller bucks. The larger bucks come last and will show up in the last few minutes of legal shooting light, or after dark.

During the "peak" of the rut (actually the pre-rut) bucks may show up a half hour, to an hour earlier, than they normally do. Depending on the weather and hunting pressure, they may also stay active the entire day in their search for a mate, though *a majority of the chasing and breeding, by mature bucks, is done after dark.*

WEATHER AND DEER ACTIVITY

Reading the Weather:

Barometric pressure measures the density of air. A rising barometer (high pressure) means fair weather and clear skies and a falling barometer (low pressure) means moisture and bad weather.

If you only have a limited amount of time available to hunt, it would be best to hunt during those times most likely to create additional deer activity and hunt in those locations where this activity is most likely to occur. By watching weather forecasts and checking your own barometer, you can determine when your chances are best.

You can get barometric information from your own barometer or get a weather radio for camp or home. These radios are permanently tuned to the National Weather Service frequency and give continual updated forecasts.

Deer and other game animals read and react to these barometric changes by their inner ears' sensitivity to changes in atmospheric pressure. *According to various studies, a deers' peak activity is generated when the barometric pressure is dropping down to between the 29 and 30+ mark.*

Deer tend to feed more right before, and a few hours after the completion of a major storm. Deer tend to move later in the morning, after bad storms and on cloudy days, and earlier in the afternoon, when it is overcast or there is an approaching storm. A barometer can foretell these activities.

For example a falling barometer, which should cause deer to begin feeding, in preparation for a stretch of bad weather, would indicate that it would be a good time to be stand hunting, near food sources, on travel lanes between food sources, or travel lanes from bedding areas to food sources.

If the barometric pressure drops below 29, this usually means a fairly serious storm is brewing and deer tend to head to bedding areas and stay tight. If you feel lucky you can try still hunting through thick security cover or heavy timber during these conditions, but the odds are definitely in favor of the deer.

Constant high or low pressure readings don't create much excitement but when these readings decide to change, the actions begins. Gradual drops or rises in barometric pressure cause action, and all game animals move more when the barometer moves up or down, but *the most activity occurs when the barometer moves quickly and especially when it falls quickly, which signals an approaching storm.*

In simple terms this means that game animals tend to feed more actively the day before, and a day or two after, a major storm hits your hunting area.

You can also watch approaching cloud systems and learn to read what they tell you about possible up coming weather situations. A red sunset usually foretells good weather and a yellow sunset or a moon with a halo or corona around it usually foretells the coming of bad weather within the next 24 hours.

A good barometer is a very important, but often overlooked, item in a hunter's bag of tricks.

Wind Reactions:

Deer activity generally decreases with increased wind velocity, especially if the wind is constantly changing directions. In very high winds deer will often times take refuge in conifer stands or old growth timber. They will also tend to bed on the leeward side of the hill approximately 1/3 of the way down, where the winds are calmest.

A strong, constant wind coming from one direction will limit deer activity and a strong gusty or swirly wind coming from several different directions makes them very jumpy. They know that during these conditions they cannot depend on their ears or their nose for protection. On days like these they like to set-up in protective cover with good visibility and just sit tight.

Temperature:

If the weather is very cold, deer will stay bedded later than usual and will tend to bed in heavy old growth timber or warmer south facing slopes.

If the weather is not too hot, deer have a high activity pattern between 10:00 and 12:00. They will move within their security cover or limited areas beyond this cover to feed, or at the least, they will get up to stretch, relieve their bowels, survey their surroundings, possibly have a few bites to eat or drink, move into or out of the sun, reposition themselves to take advantage of changing thermals or other wind patterns and then bed down again until the evening feeding time.

I shot a small three point because of this noon time movement pattern once. I was still hunting along some edge cover when I heard a couple of twigs break on the other side of a high, dense, blackberry thicket. I slowly crept along until I was able to climb up on an old dead tree trunk. This allowed me to see over the berries. As soon as I did, I saw two bucks standing in a small glade. I promptly shot the largest of the two.

Heavy Rain:

During heavy rains deer tend to stay bedded and don't move much unless spooked. But if the pre-rut is on, this rule doesn't mean much! I took a very nice 4 x 4 a few years ago during a torrential down-pour, which I had to force myself to go out and hunt in. But I was glad I did, since this buck was with seven or eight does and was more concerned with procreation than survival.

But last year I convinced myself that I wasn't going to hunt one weekend, because of the continual down-pour and I missed the two best days of the extended muzzle loader season.

I talked to two other hunters I knew, who hunted in the same area as I did, who hunted during this monsoon and they saw bucks all day long and saw several very large bucks. The bucks' sex drive over-powered their normal weather controlled activity patterns.

If you're a gambler and a good still hunter, and believe in hunting bedding areas and security cover, this is the time to do it. The deer will stay bedded longer and the rain will help cover your hunting noise.

The Rut:

The pre-rut is the time of greatest activity, since a large number of mature bucks (which are the first ones to heed natures call) try to find the first few estrous does. This pre-rut activity is brought to a frenzy when the first few cold (30 to 35 degree) days arrive. If the weather remains warm or turns warm again after a cold spell, the "peak" of the rut is extended.

When a doe first comes into estrus she will spend a pre-dominant amount of her time in one concentrated area, possibly for as long as several days. *During this time, her home range decreases but her activity level increases,* as she randomly criss-crosses her restricted habitat hoping to get the attention of an amorous buck.

A doe, who's in estrous, peak activity seems to be between 6 a.m. and 9 a.m. and 1 p.m. and 9 p.m. These activity periods are longer in duration and start earlier in the morning and afternoon than typical pre-rut activity patterns. *A buck's greatest activity, during the rut, is between 6 a.m. and 12 noon.*

Does will centralize their activity so that they are near food, water, and protective habitat. They will also try to centralize their activity near favored feeding areas and high traffic areas between feeding and bedding locations. Many times I have seen does bedded right in the feeding area or within a few yards of major deer trails. This is the one time of the year when you have a good chance of seeing a big buck on a major trail, or at least, see the signs of their activity as they search for friendly does.

Once a doe is ready to be bred, she will remain in heat for about 24 hours. If she isn't bred, and about 22 to 40 percent of does aren't bred, this first period, she will be ready to breed again in 27 to 28 days. This is what we call the second rut and generally happens around Thanksgiving, in Oregon.

Favored breeding areas are used year after year and can be identified by the high level of activity in the form of tracks and doe sightings, as well as the high percentage of buck rubs in and around the area.

Blacktail bucks are not as aggressive as whitetails and do not use scrapes, but they do rub trees. A series of rubbed trees

Photo credit: Chuck Bartlett

This doe's strategy worked!

Photo credit: Chuck Bartlett

This buck is trying to catch the scent of a doe in estrous.

in a particular area may indicate the home range or overlapping of the home ranges of one or more bucks. It may also indicate a potential "core" breeding location. These concentrated rubs are usually close to preferred bedding locations.

Prior to the breeding season, starting soon after the bucks have shed the velvet from their antlers, bucks start their sparring matches to establish dominance in the local deer population. During this time I have seen a lot of bucks, both large and small, sparring and pushing each other around to see who's boss. No one gets hurt, just some friendly pushing and shoving. This saves a lot of serious fighting once the does come into estrous.

Generally, serious fighting happens when a dominant buck from out of the area enters the territory of another dominant buck, when there are a limited number of estrous does available. Since both bucks have established dominance in their areas and are not willing to back down, they have to fight to save face and to see who is the toughest.

During the rut, if you see a doe with her tail pointing straight out, it means that she is in heat. Keep track of her if you want to bag a buck. A dominant buck that is in the rut may also walk with his tail sticking straight out, his head held high, neck extended and walk with a kind of swagger or strut. *A buck which is constantly licking his lips, is looking for a doe and is trying to increase the sensitivity of his sense of smell so he can pick up any stray doe odors on the prevailing air currents.*

Rattling:

Rattling definitely does work on blacktails if it is done at the correct time. The most effective rattling will happen with a mature deer population, and a buck to doe ratio of three or less. There is a lot of ink used in the discussion of which is the best type of antler to use for rattling, but for what it's worth, I prefer to use heavier antlers with three or more points. Some hunters prefer to cut off the ends of the antler tips, but I prefer to leave them intact. They seem to sound more realistic to me and I can create the "light sparring" sound of two bucks in a semi-serious confrontation.

If you rattle during the normal rifle or muzzle loader season you should paint your antlers a bright color and do not hunt in camouflaged clothing. There might be someone out there with an itchy trigger finger.

I personally have not had much experience with bringing in bucks while rattling. I have rattled in a couple of small bucks, but nothing big. But I know several archers who have found rattling, and rattling in conjunction with the use of a buck grunt, to be very effective and have taken several nice bucks using this technique. Archers, with their latter season dates have a better chance to hit the pre-rut and also the second rut.

I will give you some general rattling guidelines I have learned from other writers and people who I have talked to. There is even one individual who did his masters thesis on antler rattling in Texas. Most of the written information involves rattling for white tails but some of the general principles also apply to blacktails. So here goes.

1. Best times to rattle: During the pre-rut before most of the does have come into estrous, and just before the second estrous cycle of the does who were not breed earlier. In cold clear weather with a light wind. Morning time is best on days following dark nights and mid-day is best on days following moonlit nights. Most big bucks were rattled in

Photo credit: Chuck Bartlett

Two large bucks deciding who's boss!

during the pre and post-rut periods, and the largest number of true trophy bucks were seen during mid-day rattling sessions. Given the moon phase study, I would also presume that these larger bucks were rattled in during the hunters' moon.

2. Response time and actions: *Most bucks approach from down wind and most bucks respond within ten minutes, but in some cases response time takes up to 30 minutes. If you have no response within 30 minutes, move to a new location or do a new rattling sequence. Length of response time increases when you rattle during the post rut. In the Texas study, three out of 4 radio colored bucks responded to rattling, but the solo hunter located on the ground saw only 33% of these bucks.*

3. Techniques: Hunters have varied styles and these techniques work better during the different rattling cycles.

Options: Softer horn tickling generally works best during the time after which bucks become hard antlered and are establishing their dominance in the herd, but prior to the actual days before most does come into estrous. Antler tickling seems to arouse the curiosity of other bucks and they come in to see what's new in the neighborhood.

Style A: Start soft and then progressively harder. Do two or three sessions for 30 seconds to a couple of minutes then put down antlers and watch for 20 to 30 minutes. Do two or three sessions. *Style B:* Start loud and then get quieter. Do two or three sessions and then wait for 20 to 30 minutes.

You don't slam the antlers together as much you grind and rub them together vigorously. *My personal preference would be the quieter style, because knock down, drag out fights, between blacktail bucks rarely happen.*

Use doe in heat scent in a spray bottle and release it into the air while rattling, or possibly set up some scent drag lines leading near to your location.

4. How to set up: *If you're by yourself, set up in heavy cover, so that the buck can't see you and has to come closer. Be sure that you have a clear line of vision downwind of your location.* Set up near known bedding or breeding areas or security cover. Don't walk in on the trail or come in from the direction you expect the buck to approach from. *Don't expect to bring a smart old buck out into an open area or across an open area. Set up so that the buck can approach your position with enough cover so that he will feel protected.*

5. Best set-up: *Two people, with the person doing the rattling on the ground and the person doing the shooting up in an elevated stand approximately 40 or 50 yards down wind of the person doing the rattling.* 2nd best: Same scenario as above only the shooter is down wind and on the ground in heavy cover with more open cover between him and the rattler. 3rd: Solo rattler in an elevated stand. 4th: Solo rattler on the ground in heavy cover with some visibility downwind.

Wind:

Deer are controlled by their stomachs, but how they get to the locations where they satisfy their hunger is controlled by the wind, and their path of movement is determined by the topography of the land and any natural or manmade barriers!

But since there is usually a wide selection of food locations to choose from, food is of secondary importance in determining specific deer movement patterns.

What is of primary importance, in trying to out-fox a smart, old buck, is wind direction.

Wind direction, either the prevailing winds or in low wind velocity situations, the normal thermal air movement (hot air rises and cool air falls) control how a buck will reach a particular feeding or bedding location or whether the buck will use it all. *ALL MOVEMENT IS DETERMINED BY THE DIRECTION OF THE WIND!*

It is my belief that the major reason for the blacktails unpredictable behavior, in the form of travel and feeding habits is the wide variety of available food sources, food locations, and changing wind patterns.

I constantly read about large mature whitetails using the same trails or travel patterns over and over, if undisturbed. Not so the average mature blacktail. Disturbed or not, he has a very variable activity pattern.

During the summer months wind patterns are more predictable, but Oregon's fall weather is continually changing. Wind patterns are further complicated by the varied terrain which changes and redirects air movement and thus deer movement.

The years in which I have seen the largest number of large bucks and where I have seen the same buck more than once during the hunting season, are years where the weather and wind patterns remained fairly constant over a period of consecutive days.

Bucks use the wind when they bed and will bed below the top of the ridge so that the prevailing wind will warn them of immediate danger on their back trail. Rising thermals, if not canceled out by the prevailing winds, will carry scents from below and their eyes will also search for danger from below and further down their back trail.

The thermal reversal (hot air rises) takes place once the sun has sufficiently warmed the earth's surface, somewhere around 9:00 to 10:00 in the morning, unless it is overridden by prevailing wind or weather conditions. At this time the air flow will change from a downward to an upward direction.

In the evening the thermals will reverse themselves again as the temperature cools and air begins to travel down hill. *Deer will change their bedding locations depending on the weather and changes in temperature and wind currents.*

Deer Trails:

Wind shapes, and geography directs deer trails. Deer follow the rule of the "path of least resistance". This means that under normal non-threatening situations, deer will always follow the easiest travel route, which has the lowest visibility or greatest cover. During daylight hours they travel below the ridge line and cross over at natural saddles, through swales, or at the point where the ridge point begins to taper off. This provides visual screening and protection while giving them visibility into the next drainage, basin, or similar habitat, before they actually move into it.

They will follow the natural terrain, keeping to the low spots and heavier vegetation for concealment, and higher sheltered locations for visibility into the next valley or swale.

You can direct the travel of deer to a limited degree by blocking off trails with natural vegetation or opening up trails through heavy cover.

Escape trails are distinguished by the fact that they generally are not set up for line of sight visibility, lead into heavy cover, do not necessarily follow the lay of the land but they do cover the shortest distance between two points. They begin and disappear randomly and do not go very far.

Good escape trail locations are off the points of finger ridges, between known bedding habitat and heavy security cover, and cross country cross over trails, between normal trails.

To learn how deer move through their natural surroundings, follow their daytime trails over varied terrain and learn how they use the natural topography to their advantage.

In areas where there are fences, look for crossing locations. Sure, a deer can simply jump a four or five foot fence, but the fact of the matter is, that they prefer to go under or cross where the fence has been lowered by a fallen tree, old broken wire or adjacent topography.

Once you have followed and studied several of these travel routes you will put life and vision into your study of new areas and your use of topo maps and aerial photos, and you will be able to make good guesses as to the potential travel, bedding, and various feeding possibilities in your area of choice.

Deer will travel from bedding locations to feeding locations in the evening with the prevailing wind at their backs, and will return to hillside bedding locations in the morning with the prevailing wind in their face or crosswise to their line of travel. Most trails are not bi-directional and travel only in one direction either to or from bedding or feeding areas.

It has been shown that does teach their trail and travel patterns to their fawns. This is why it is unwise to give away your presence by sight, scent, and sound to any deer which you see while stand hunting. If there are repeated disturbances, the does will avoid the area and may even teach their young to avoid the area.

Body Language:

If a deer suddenly funnels both of its ears in the same direction and turns its head in the same direction, it means that it has heard something and is trying to confirm it's hearing with its sight before deciding what to do.

If a deer begins a head bob routine it means that it has noticed something it is uncomfortable with and is trying to get more confirmation before reacting.

This is not the time to make any unnecessary movement. If the deer gets no further confirmation it may go back to feeding or it will begin a stiff legged walk, like it's walking on eggs. This may turn into a stiff legged trot or a low headed sneak, with tail tucked between its legs, or it may develop into a full-fledged flight, with white flag flying and high bounding leaps.

When alerted, a doe may blow and snort or stomp her foot as a warning to other deer. A buck may snort, but he will usually not do any foot stomping. He is quicker to take flight than a doe. Unlike the doe which instinctively tries to alert her fawns or other deer of danger, a buck's first sense of duty is to himself. He simply wants to fade out of sight with the least commotion possible.

If a deer lays its ears back, it's ready to run. Shoot now or forget it. If a deer's tail is relaxed, pointed downward and moving lazily from side to side, all is well. If the deer's tail stops moving or the deer suddenly tenses up it tells you that the deer's acute senses have picked up something that concerns it. It has not identified exactly what it is yet, but it knows something is wrong.

A deer is nervous when it's feeding, because it knows that its hearing and sight are limited, so it will pop up its head every few seconds to check out the scenery. If it is alerted, not only will it rotate its eyes upward while feeding, but it will pretend to put its head down to feed and them immediately pop it up again. Thereby hoping to catch you or another predator while it's moving.

If a deer picks up its head, directs its eyes and ears in your direction, and then tenses up its body, the game is over!! In female deer, this may be followed by its raising one front leg and then bringing it strongly down to the ground two or three times before it starts to run. *Any form of tensing up of a deer's body is a sign that it has sensed that something is wrong!*

If the deer is alerted but not yet spooked, *slowly* bring your gun or bow to a shooting position. Only move quickly if the deer is already moving. I do not recommend taking running shots with a bow or a muzzle loader and I caution against taking quick shots at running game, with a rifle.

A smaller buck will keep its head down and will sometimes put its tail between its legs when a dominate buck approaches or is in the same area.

Telemetric Studies:

Telemetric studies tell us that bucks stay on the periphery of the does' favored habitat during the summer months and then move into them during the rut. They also tell us that Saturday has the least trail usage during the hunting season and that Monday, Tuesday and Wednesday have the greatest.

Photo credit: Chuck Bartlett

This bucks body language tells you he knows somethings up!

These studies also show that deer are not creatures of habit, as they only used consecutive trails on two consecutive days about 25% of the time. These studies are in line with what I have observed during my hunting time. A deer's repeated use of any particular trail is controlled by wind direction and therefore gets varied use.

According to telemetric studies, bucks are more active between 3 p.m. and 9 p.m. on evenings with a full moon. When the moon is a 1/4 moon to no moon, then the greatest activity is from 6 a.m. to 9 a.m.

Deer return to their beds about 30 minutes later and leave their beds about 15 minutes earlier on cloudy days. On sunny, clear days they return to their beds only a few minutes after sunrise and leave their beds just before sunset.

Undisturbed deer acting in their normal cycle will bed for one to three hours at a time and will actually spend about 70% of their time bedded. Obviously, mature deer or deer in heavy hunting pressure situations may stay bedded for longer periods of time. We, as hunters, need to take all of this available information and apply it to the specific circumstances and locations where we choose to hunt.

Chapter 12

Of Guns, Bows and Optics

Ballistic Information, Weapon Selection, How to choose the right optics.

I have enlarged this section and created another new section which was not in my previous book because I've realized that if you supply people with information to allow them to hunt more effectively, *it is critical that you also instill in them the importance of a well-placed shot, the necessity for careful follow up, and give them the tools to effectively find the animal which they have shot!*

If you follow the general principles noted in this chapter you will have a good knowledge of the basics needed to be a safe, effective hunter.

If you don't practice with your weapon, so that you can shoot accurately, if you don't know how to judge distances correctly or how to use a range finder, and if you do not know the ballistics, trajectory and capabilities of your gun or bow, you should not be out in the woods hunting!!!

GUNS

Choose a gun you are comfortable with, which fits you and brings up easily and naturally. If the gun feels awkward, do not buy it unless you plan on reworking it yourself, or having it reworked by a competent gunsmith.

Check out the trigger pull. If it pulls hard or unevenly take it to a local gunsmith to be adjusted. A good trigger pull should have a steady, even pull so that you do not know when the rifle is ready to go off. Don't mess with this yourself, as too light a trigger pull can be potentially dangerous.

Study ballistic and trajectory tables, then shoot enough to see how your gun actually shoots at various distances. If you are the average shooter (and I put myself in that category), you should know exactly where your gun shoots, from 25 to 200 yards. Don't try to shoot longer than these distances, and *any distance over 100 yards should be done with a rest, not offhand, and no shots at running game!*

A pellet gun makes an excellent under study weapon if you live far from a rifle range or an area where it is hard to find a place to shoot. If city or county codes do not prohibit it, you can even set up a small, targeted back drop at your home. Distance is not important here. What you are practicing is bringing up the rifle, holding it steady, and slowly pulling the trigger. If you have developed a flinch, like I have, using a pellet gun should break you of this habit.

When you're hunting don't rush the shot; your first one is usually your best, carefully squeeze, don't jerk the trigger! As mentioned above, if the animal is spotted beyond 100 yards, it would be best to practice your stalking skills to try and close the distance, rather than attempting to "stretch your barrel."

I do not recommend taking long shots in low light situations, where additional time will be needed to reach the shot location and track the animal. This just increases the percentage for lost game.

The longest shot I have ever taken on a blacktail deer was 185 steps but the majority of my shots have been much closer. Since 1981, my longest shot at a blacktail deer is 60 yards. *Know your gun's limitations and then hunt within the gun's, and your own shooting abilities!*

Sight in your gun at a rifle range, with measured distances, before every hunting season. If you do not intend to take shots over 100 yards then sight in your rifle to be on at 25 yards, which puts it an inch or so high at 50, and back on again at about 100 yards. If you think you will be shooting at distances over 100 yards and you have practiced such shots, then sight in your rifle to be three inches high at 100 yards. You should check your individual rifle ballistics and also check it out at the rifle range, but this should put your bullet back on target at between 200 and 250 yards.

If the deer is above or below you, a behind the shoulder shot at these distances will work with no needed adjustment for gravity. Hunters typically tend to overshoot game except at distances where they should not be shooting anyway.

I'm strongly in favor of using a good quality scope, but do not use your scope to view unknown objects. That's what your binoculars are for, since binoculars do not have triggers attached to them, which can accidently go off and kill someone!

With an unloaded gun, practice bringing your rifle up quickly to your shoulder and aiming at a predetermined target. With practice you should be able to immediately "get on target" as soon as the rifle comes to your shoulder. Do this until it becomes second nature to you. Practice this with your hunting clothing on to be sure that the rifle will work, as it should in actual hunting situations.

When you bring the rifle to your shoulder you should immediately see the entire sight picture without having to adjust your head. If you don't have a quick, clear sight picture, adjust the comb of the rifle where your cheek hits the stock, adjust the height of your scope mounts or shorten or lengthen your stock. If you don't feel comfortable doing these adjustments yourself, take yourself and your rifle to a competent gunsmith and explain what you need to accomplish. Let him do the rest.

Please remember in all of this, that *I am not advocating quick, hasty shots, only quick responses. Never shoot unless you're sure of what and where you are shooting and confident of your ability to kill the animal cleanly!!! The average bullet will travel 3,000 to 4,000 feet before it runs out of energy. So even if you miss the animal you're shooting at, you always have the possibility of hitting something or someone else before your bullet runs out of energy!!*

When you're out in the woods, hiking, camping or scouting, practice estimating distances. Measure your stride and pace off the distance, or better yet, purchase one of the new laser range finders. Bushnell makes a good one at a very affordable price for rifle hunters (I personally prefer the compact 600 series) and even has one that fits on a bow. Ranging also makes several range finders specifically for bow hunters.

Given the "cost" of losing a wounded game animal or missing the trophy of a life-time, the cost of a reasonably priced range finder should not be a factor. On the other hand, if we keep our rifle shots to under 100 yards and our archery shots to 20 to 25 yards, we will have no need for a range finder.

A well-sighted in rifle, a well-tuned bow, and practice at estimating distances is all we need. Except, of course, the ability to control our rapidly beating heart and our all too common, cases of "buck fever."

Learn the size of the animal you are hunting so you know what it looks like at various distances.

Game across a draw or canyon will seem further away than it is, while a silhouetted deer will seem closer than it is. When you see only part of a game animal it will seem further away than it actually is.

Game seen in low light situations, foggy weather and overcast days, will also seem further away. On the other hand, on clear days game may seem closer than it actually is and game sighted on level, open ground will also appear closer than it actually is. This last situation is something we normally don't have to worry about with blacktail deer!

RULES OF THE ROAD: *Never change bullet weights or bullet manufacturers, without resighting in your rifle. If you drop your rifle, take a bad fall, or jar your scope, be sure and test your rifle to make sure that it is still on target. If you've fallen, also check to make sure that your barrel isn't plugged with debris, before firing it. Before entering the woods always check to make sure that your variable scope is set to the correct power, which typically in blacktail country, is its lowest setting.*

I have heard of stories of too many game animals being missed or wounded because hunters had changed bullets without resighting in their rifle, or they encountered game at very close range, only to find that their scope was at high power, and all the shooter could see was hair.

I went hunting once without checking my scope, which had been jarred when it fell from its rest on the side of my truck. It was a short fall and I didn't think much about it. Later in the day I had a chance for a frontal neck shot at a buck from a distance of only about 30 or 40 yards. I put the crosshairs on the spot where the neck joins the chest and fired. At my shot the deer did not move, much less drop dead. Since he didn't flinch I decided that my rifle must be shooting high. I lowered my cross hairs to the bottom of the deer's brisket, giving myself a large vertical target line and fired again. At the shot the deer dropped instantly with a bullet in the neck. My rifle was shooting about 10″ high.

If you hunt with a bullet in the chamber, make sure that your safety is on; never hunt with your finger on the trigger. It should go without saying, that you should absolutely never, ever, point your rifle at another person and you should never take a loaded rifle into car, camp or home!

Fortunately I have not heard of any personal stories, where hunters have been injured from careless gun handling, but I was walking ahead of another hunter once, who had his finger on the trigger of his rifle, while his safety was off, and I still vividly remember the sound of his rifle going off and the foot deep crater in the dirt, caused by his bullet, only a few inches behind my right foot. On another occasion, when I was younger, I watched some road hunters drive up to a large clear cut during the doe season, and in the excitement of trying to quickly get out of their vehicle, to get a shot at a doe, their loaded rifle went off and the bullet shattered their front windshield. They were very lucky that no one was injured, as there were three people in the front of the truck when the rifle went off.

Whenever you shoot at a game animal, even if you think that you missed, or believe that the deer didn't show any sign of a hit, you should always carefully and thoroughly *follow up every shot to be sure that it was either a hit or a miss. In fact, your state of mind should be that you hit the deer until proven otherwise!*

Because of the great importance of this procedure I will devote an entire chapter to checking your shot and trailing wounded game.

Most of the time, deer will show no sign of a hit or at least no reactions that the average hunter will notice. There is no excuse for not using every means you have to follow up a wounded animal. *Be sure and memorize where the deer was when you shot by locating an easily identifiable landmark, and also mark the spot you shot from.*

I'm a firm believer in the "more lead is better" philosophy, when it comes to wounded game. If the deer doesn't drop at the first shot and you have time and can *safely* put another bullet or arrow into the animal you should. It's better to ruin a little meat than lose an entire animal or make it suffer needlessly.

Last season a friend of mine and his son were hunting together, when he shot a nice buck which dropped instantly at the shot. But while they were high fiveing and congratulating each other on the shot, the buck got up and ran away.

Even a critically wounded deer can still travel several hundred yards and further, and *once the deer gets out of our sight our advantage is lost.*

If there isn't a heavy blood trail, and most times even with well-placed shots there isn't, it is very easy to lose the track of a wounded animal in the heavy cover typical of blacktail deer habitat. Add an indistinct trail, heavy cover, other intersecting trails, the commingling of other fresh tracks, or on-coming darkness or rain and the problems increase dramatically.

So when you shoot an animal, even if it does down immediately, watch it for a few minutes, with gun ready to make sure that it doesn't get up or crawl off. If it shows any signs of life or starts to get up, shoot it again!

A lot of "dead" deer have gotten up and escaped after they were knocked down and presumed to be dead! Don't assume anything! If you're hunting with a partner have one person cover the deer while the other one goes over to where the deer is, being careful not to be in the other hunter's line of fire. The person approaching the deer should also have his (her) rifle loaded and ready as they approach the "dead deer".

In the discussion of rifle calibers, don't believe that big is better, nor believe that any rifle can do the job well "if you just hit them right". Just because Grandpa Jones,"the world's best hunter", used a 30-30 with open sights does not mean that you should do the same. Just because old Uncle Earl would use nothing less than a 300 HH Weatherby Magnum does not mean that you should follow suit. Ask for different hunter's opinions, read all of the gun and ammo books you can, and then make your own decision. Each person has a favorite weapon and you should take time to determine yours.

There has been a lot of paper used up writing about what is the best load for hunting in brush, but I found a recent article very informative. This author tested a wide variety of rifle calibers and bullets for their "brush busting" capabilities by placing 3/8" and 1/4" wooden dowels in front of his target to simulate shooting through heavy vegetation. The rifles he used were all of the typical calibers, plus a few unusual ones.

He found that even though pointed bullets have a flatter trajectory and retain more energy over long distances, round or flat nosed bullets tend to track better and have *less* tendency to key-hole, when shot through brush. *But he found that all of the bullets' effective killing power were reduced, after they made contact with the dowels.*

This shows us that it is not a good idea to shoot at game animals screened by brush. *Look for an opening to shoot through or don't shoot. The chances of wounding game are too high!*

You should match the type of bullet to the game you hunt, using a faster-expanding, lighter grained bullet on thin-skinned game, like deer, and a heavier grained bullet on thicker-skinned game, such as elk. A 140 to 150 grain bullet is fine for deer.

It is not the ballistics of the gun which causes success or failure, it's the person pulling the trigger. Try never to let the excitement of the moment overcome the placement of the shot. Control your excitement. If it's a buck, don't concentrate on the antlers, but instead, concentrate on specific shot placement. If your rifle is not steady, wait until it is!

I started hunting with a 6.5 Swedish Military Mauser which was hand loaded by my step-grandfather. It was an excellent rifle and served its purpose well. When I got older

Photo credit: Chuck Bartlett

Take your time. Any game animal is much too good to waste or wound, with a careless shot.

I purchased an old remodeled 30-06 Springfield. This rifle also fulfilled its purpose.

I currently use a lightweight 7mm 08, which I originally purchased for a back packing trip I had planned for Sitka Blacktail in Alaska. After I purchased the rifle, I had Larry Brace, a local gunsmith and serious blacktail hunter, set the trigger pull, so that it was just right.

This is certainly more rifle than I need, for my style of blacktail hunting, but it is so light and easy to carry, I now use it for all my deer hunting and I doubt that I will ever have a need for another rifle.

I believe that the average hunter, and I put myself in that category, is better off, if he or she uses one gun for most, if not all of his big game hunting, so he or she will become intimately familiar with how it operates and shoots. I have seen hunters miss chances at deer because they had recently changed rifles and were unfamiliar with how the new gun functioned.

To protect your rifle barrel during rainy or snowy weather or in the case of an accidental fall, which could cause an obstruction, cover the end, of the barrel, with a small balloon. This will not affect the rifles accuracy or ballistics.

Shots at Running Deer:

THE FIRST GENERAL RULE WOULD BE, DON'T!!! For the average hunter, any shot at running game over 50 yards away should not be taken, and shots at running game at any distance should be avoided. Even at 50 yards the hunter needs to swing with the animal, as in skeet shooting, to place the bullet correctly.

Most of us did not grow up like Jack O'Connor, shooting running jack rabbits in the sagebrush territory of Texas and Arizona. In fact we did not grow up with any experience at shooting running game and *without lots of experience, hitting running or moving game, is a matter of "pure luck" not "pure skill".*

As a point of interest, many times you can stop a running deer, with a shrill whistle or a loud squeal, similar to a predator call or a doe or fawn distress call. They won't stop long and they may not stop in the open, but more times than not, they will stop!

A deer running on level unobstructed terrain can reach 30 to 40 miles per hour, but in typical hunting situations it will be closer to 20 to 30 miles per hour. A trotting deer will be traveling six to eight miles per hour and a walking deer still is traveling about three miles per hour.

At 100 yards a walking deer will travel about six to nine inches in the time it takes the average 150 gr. bullet pushed at 2900 ft. per. second to reach it. (A 7mm-08 with a 145 gr. bullet at 2900 f.p.s. will cover 100 yards in .108 seconds) A trotting or bounding deer will travel about 12 to 15 inches in the same time, and a deer running at about 30 miles per hour will have traveled 4.4 feet in this time.

These calculations are only figured for 100 yards. At further distances the time for the bullet to reach the target increases disproportionately because the bullet is slowing down faster, the further it is away from the rifle.

Let's analyze, for the fun of it, the story a hunter recently told you about shooting a running deer, at over three hundred yards, and hitting it exactly where he or she planned, in the neck or right behind the shoulder.

At three hundred yards, depending on rifle caliber, bullet speed and weight, shape and sectional density, the typical big game rifle, sighted in to shoot three inches high at 100 yards, will hit seven to sixteen inches below the point of aim. At the same distance with a 20 mph cross wind, the bullet will drift 10 to 20 inches, or up to 40 inches, if the bullet is our great grandfather's flat nosed 170 gr. 30 - 30. Given a light, 10 m.p.h. cross wind, the bullet drift will still be eight to ten inches.

When the leaves are rustling in the trees this equates to a 10 m.p.h. wind. If the branches are bending and moving slightly or there are ripples on the water, the wind is traveling 10 to 15 m.p.h.. When the trees are bending and there are whitecaps on the water, then this equates to a 25 to 30 plus m.p.h. wind.

At 300 hundred yards, a running deer will have traveled about 10 to 13 feet by the time your bullet reaches him, or again about 29 to 30 feet, if the bullet is shot from grandpa's old 30-30.

If the shooter wobbles slightly or jerks the trigger and causes the rifle to move, say even 1/8 of an inch, at the time of the shot, this will create a 35 to 45 inch variation in point of impact vs point of aim! Also, by the time the bullet gets out to 300 yards, due to the effects of gravity, your 2900 f.p.s. bullet is only traveling about 2100 f.p.s., and because of this decreased velocity your expansion capabilities, i.e. knock down power and penetration, have been reduced dramatically.

So to hit a running deer at 300 yards, in a stiff breeze, a hunter would have to release a perfect, undisturbed off hand shot, aiming about 7 to 16 inches high, and somewhere between 11 to 15 feet in front of the animal, to compensate for speed, distance, and wind velocity, all the while having his rifle follow through ahead of the moving animal, to compensate for the time between the time the brain says to fire and the finger actually pulls the trigger. He would also have to estimate correctly the deer's line of travel, 11 to 15 feet in advance, know whether the bucks zigging or zagging, and know whether the deer would be sailing through the air at this time, or be at the bottom of his jump, screened or unscreened by vegetation, and various other considerations.

All of which obviously shows that unless the hunter has just won the Olympic shooting championship or some other similar prestigious moving marksmanship award, luck is the only element that allowed him or her to kill the animal and luck should have nothing to do with our use of a rifle while shooting at game!!!

OPTICS

Buy the best optics you can afford, keeping in mind that the most expensive does not necessarily mean the best, but also that cheap optics are never worth the money! The quality of all optics has increased tremendously over the years.

When looking at scopes and binoculars, be sure and compare the clarity of the lens and visibility in low light situations, not just during common day-light situations.

I prefer a seven power binocular and I prefer a variable scope, though to be honest, now that I always carry binoculars I seldom change the scope setting above 3 power. I currently use a lightweight 3 x 9 x 36 Swarovski AL on my 7mm-08 and a 3 x 9 x 43 Leupold Vari X III on my .280 back up rifle. There are many good high quality optics available, so carefully shop and compare.

The light gathering ability of scopes and binoculars is dependent on the size of the objective, the quality of the glass and glass coating and the exit pupil size. The exit pupil size is obtained by dividing the objective size by the magnification.

The light gathering ability of various objectives is disproportionate, in that a 50mm objective does not transmit twice the amount of light as a 25mm objective lens, it transmits four times the amount of light!!

The ideal exit pupil size is between 5m and 7m, which matches the size of the eye's pupil in normal to dark light situations. An exit pupil larger than this does no good because the eye cannot take advantage of this extra light. *Make sure that all of the optics on your scope and binocular are fully multi-coated to minimize glare and increase light gathering ability. All of the better well-known name brands have coated optics.*

A high quality pair of light-gathering binoculars and a rifle scope is a must. My 3 x 9 x 36 Swarovski scope has an exit pupil of 12 at three power, and four at nine power, and my 3 x 9 x 43 Leupold scope have an exit pupil of 14.3 at three, and 4.77 at nine power. At the mid-range power of 6, my scopes have a 6 and 7.16 exit pupil respectively.

I have never used anything above three power while hunting blacktails and I have only used the six power setting once, while hunting mule deer. Both of these scopes have the ability to convey more light at the low to mid setting than our eyes have the ability to use.

The comparison as to which scope is actually best in low light will depend on the quality of the lenses and whether the lenses are fully multi-coated.

Binoculars which are best for low light situations are the larger models, such as the 7 x 50's, the 8 x 56's or 10 x 50's. *Other than the quality and the light transmitting ability of the optics, the two most important items are the binocular's exit pupil size and the twilight factor.* The twilight factor is obtained by multiplying the diameter of the objective lens (the lens furthest from your eye) by the magnification power of the binocular and then finding the square root of this figure. A 8 x 56 or 10 x 50 binocular would have an exit pupil of seven and five respectively (divide the objective lens size by the binoculars power), and a 7 x 50 would have an exit pupil size of 7.14. The twilight factor of the 7 x 50's would be 18.7 while the twilight factor of the 8 x 56 binoculars would be 21.2 and the twilight factor of the 10 x 50's would be 22.4. By this comparison the 8 x 56's and the 10 x 50's would provide the greatest amount of visibility in dim light situations.

But I have found that the 8 x 56's and 10 x 50 binoculars are too much magnification for short range hunting, so if you feel that most of your hunting is going to be at close range, then a better choice would be the 7 x 50's. I have a pair of 7 x 50 Swarovski's which function great, even in very heavy cover. These binoculars allow me to see into and through vegetation, which with my normal eyesight,

Photo credit: Chuck Bartlett

Now's the time for a pair of good light gathering binoculars!

seems to be an impenetrable tangle. You won't believe how much more you can see until you try it!

The small compacts are light and easy to carry but are useless during dim light situations. It is during these times when you have the best chance of shooting a large trophy buck.

Which binocular would you rather have when a smart, old buck pokes his nose out of the dim shadows at dusk: A small, light weight, compact version, which lets you see only slightly better in low light situations than your existing eyesight or a big heavy pair of binoculars which lets you know what you're looking at? Point made??

Everything else being equal, a porro-prism binocular is cheaper to produce and has more light gathering ability than an equally priced roof-prism but porro-prism binoculars are bulkier and roof prisms are more sleek and compact in design.

Always check the wording associated with the lens of your binoculars since things are not always as they seem. The words "coated optics" means only that at least one of the lenses is coated, "fully-coated" means all surfaces have a single coating, "multi-coated" means at least one lens has multiple coatings and "fully-multicoated" means that there are at least two coatings on all lenses. The last would be the best, because with "fully- multicoated" lenses you should get 80% to 95% light transmission off the internal lenses.

When you use large heavy optics it is a good idea to purchase a wide comfortable neck strap and a securing strap. I think that Butler Creek makes the best neck strap on the market. See product information chapter entitled Gizmos and Gadgets.

Next you need to decide on some system to secure the binoculars to your chest to keep them from flopping around and thereby causing unneeded noise, movement and additional neck strain. I have developed a simple inexpensive chest support which works well for me and I can use it with all of my different binoculars. In case you're interested, I will include information on my chest strap in the chapter entitled "Gizmos and Gadgets".

There are also several other binocular securing straps on the market which you can look at. *But one thing is for certain and that is, if you decide to use binoculars, you need to use one of these securing straps, or you will quit using binoculars! Without the use of the appropriate straps, the binoculars will become only a heavy burden around your neck, will always be in the way or catching on something, or will be constantly causing noise related problems!*

Also, when you use binoculars it is best to use a gun or bow sling which will allow you to keep your weapon ready and allow you to use your binoculars without having to put your rifle or bow down on the ground or rest them against something.

Safari Sling makes an excellent rifle strap for this purpose. Information about this company is listed in the "Gizmos and Gadgets" chapter of this book. I have seen a couple of bow slings advertised, but I have no knowledge about them, so all you archers out there will have to do your own research.

If you want your optics to treat you well then you must treat them well!!! Keep them covered with protective covers except when hunting. Butler Creek makes some excellent flip-up binocular and scope covers. Never wipe your binocular or scope with your shirt or kleenex and do not fog them with your breath before cleaning. Use a liquid anti-fogging, anti-static, cleaning solution with professional cleaning tissue. Prior to using the lens cleaning liquid and lens cleaning tissue, use an air gun or camel hair blower brush to clear the lens of dust particles, which will scratch the lens and damage the protective covering on the lens. Also, do not put excessive pressure on the lens tissue when cleaning and do not clean with liquids and lens tissue more than needed. Many times the air gun or camel hair brush blower brush is all that is needed.

North American Marketing makes an excellent anti-static, anti-fogging, cleaning solution and Leupold & Stevens makes a great lens cleaning brush. Again, information on how to obtain all of these products will be covered in the chapter entitled "Gizmos and Gadgets".

Never touch the lens with your bare hands or get gun cleaning oil or solvents on the lens. This will dissolve the protective lens coating. You have paid good hard-earned money to purchase a fine, carefully manufactured piece of equipment, so treat it that way! Don't negate its usefulness by treating it carelessly.

ARCHERY

I respect the sport and I have done some bow hunting in the past, but for the present I choose to hunt with a rifle. There are still a lot more variables which affect the success of an archery hunter, even when the game is finally in sight. Plus it is my belief that there are additional chances of wounding and not recovering game with a poorly placed arrow. No, I am not saying that archers wound more deer than rifle hunters or that there are numerous deer in the woods running around with arrows in them. Responsible hunters in both camps most likely shoot and recover the same percentage of game animals.

But I personally prefer clean, quick, instantaneous kills and a rifle gives me this potential. I generally hunt in the evening and it is usually during the part of the season when there is a high probability of rain. When I finally see the deer which I want to shoot, I don't want to take a chance of missing him, having to track him in the dark or having his trail washed out by rain. A well-placed bullet in the neck at the very close distances which are common to my hunting techniques, solves these problems and puts the buck down instantly. *For me the hunt is more important than the weapon!*

I will say no more, other than to encourage you to choose the hunting method that fits your personality and then become as proficient with that weapon as you can. If you do decide to choose archery you must spend a lot of time practicing (in fact it should be a year-round situation) so that you can consistently place your arrow in the killing zone. For me this would mean shooting at *unmarked* distances, and practicing until I can consistently place my arrows in the vital zone on a full size game target, with no convenient circle, for at least five out of six shots. For most archers this would mean limiting your shots to 20 yards or under. Always match your arrows to your bow and keep your broadheads razor sharp.

It is my opinion that the consistent killing of large bucks is harder with a bow, given the many variables which can affect the final placement of the arrow. But archers are able to hunt during the early season when bucks are most active, as they consume large quantities of food used for the maturation of their antlers and also during the latter part of the season when the bucks enter the rut. This does give the archery hunter a strong advantage over the rifle hunter. In fact, at one time a bow hunter by the name of George Shurtleff held the world record blacktail record, in the Boone and Crockett, as well as the Pope and Young, scoring systems.

The hunting techniques described in this book work effectively for both bow and rifle hunting. *Only two of the last 15 to 20 bucks which I have shot, had any idea of my presence. The blacktail bucks which I have killed in the last 17 years have been taken at distances of from six to sixty steps and the buck taken at 60 steps was taken while still hunting.* The bucks which were killed at the 35 to 40 step distances would have come closer, except I became too excited and didn't give them a chance. The buck that was taken at 6 steps was actually closer than that earlier, but I had to let him pass me before I raised my rifle for the shot!! This isn't said to brag or boast, it's simply said to show how well the techniques described in this book work for me and can work for you.

Chapter 13

The Buck Stops Here!!

Successful Tactics for
Trailing Wounded Game

Though we all hope it will never happen, the fact is that eventually we, or someone we hunt with, will wound a game animal, and we owe it to the animal to make our *best effort* to retrieve that animal.

Our first *best effort* though, should be to do our best to *not make quick or poorly placed shots. Know your capabilities and hunt within them!* Also, before you go hunting, carefully study a deer's anatomy so you know where the vital organs are located, at various angles.

WHAT TO DO AFTER THE SHOT

The first rule, once the shot has been taken, would be to check out every shot we, or someone else with us, has taken *to confirm that it was not a miss. Most wounded game is lost because of a lack of follow-up and persistence, moving too quickly without adequate attention to detail, as it relates to sign or actual sightings of game, or too many well intentioned, but unknowing people muddying the water.*

If the deer does not drop instantly (and they rarely do) try to get another shot into the animal. Don't worry about losing a little meat, worry instead about losing the entire animal or causing prolonged pain and suffering. *Keep the animal's line of travel in sight for as long as you can and memorize the last place you saw the deer and its direction of travel.*

Once the deer is no longer visible, remember the reactions of the deer after the shot, the direction of travel, and exactly where it was when you shot, and where it disappeared from your view. Also, listen to see if you can determine the direction of travel from the sounds that the animal makes.

After the shot, while you continue to visually look for the animal or in the case of a downed animal while you watch to make sure that it's down for the count, wait a few minutes and let your heart rate and blood pressure settle down, so if needed, you can do a good methodical job of tracking. Take your time and act like Sherlock Holmes or Perry Mason; get all the evidence available. Move slowly and have your rifle ready. BE PATIENT!!! BE PERSISTENT!!!

Recall your sight picture and remember the deer's reactions. Recheck your shot with rifle raised to see if there was any deflecting vegetation. *But remember that a game animal doesn't necessarily give any sign of a hit, especially if the animal is already running when shot.*

I shot a spike elk once running across an open meadow toward me at a slight angle. I put the first shot behind his shoulder at about 75 yards, another one behind his shoulder when he was even with me, and I put another one behind his front shoulder when he was about 75 yards past me. There was no reaction to any of my shots until the last one, which dropped him, though all were fatal shots.

After the shot, locate a distinct, easily identifiable landmark near where the deer was standing when you shot and also where you last saw the animal. An old snag, an unusual shaped stump, a particularly odd shaped tree or branch, anything that will help you remember the *exact spot.*

Remember that things never look the same when you get to where you believe the deer was, and things also never look the same when you reach the spot and try to look back to where you shot. *So before you leave, mark clearly, and exactly the spot where your shot was taken!* Fluorescent surveyors' tape works great for this. I always carry a partial roll in my pack or pocket.

If the deer dropped in its tracks, at the shot, watch it for four or five minutes to be sure that it's down for good. A lot of "dead deer" have suddenly come back to life and escaped.

If you're hunting with a partner, have one person stay at the shot location and the other go over to the downed animal, or the location where the animal was when the shot was taken or last seen. Both hunters should keep their guns ready and one hunter should proceed quietly and carefully over to the animal. If the animal does get up, the hunter staying at the shot location should know exactly where the other hunter is and be sure there is no danger if he decides to shoot again.

It is critical to know *exactly* where the animal was standing when you shot, because this is where you will find the first evidence to help determine where the animal was hit.

TRACKING WOUNDED GAME

Once you are at the shot location, look for type, color and location of blood, pieces of bone or other body parts, pieces of hair or any other information you find which will later help you locate the animal. If you find bone fragments it usually means a rib, sternum or leg shot. Inspect and save any pieces of bone found. If you find lots of dark colored blood or frothy blood, the deer should be dead only a few yards away, but this is no reason to be careless or do a shabby job of tracking, because deer can be and are lost even when they only travel a few yards. In fact they're lost even when they don't move at all because hunters don't take the time to identify the deer's exact location or their shooting location, before leaving to find the animal.

If you do not find signs of a hit, look also for signs of a miss, i.e., a broken branch in the bullets line of travel, a bullet hole in ground, a chipped rock, etc.

Bright red blood indicates a muscle or artery wound, pink and frothy blood means a lung shot, dark deep red, a liver shot and a greenish or brownish color, a paunch or abdomen shot. This last color is the one color of blood we hope never to see, because a deer shot in this part of his anatomy can travel for miles and live for several days unless stopped with a follow up shot. Lots of blood and blood located in spurts would indicate a heart shot animal.

When you find hair, look at the color. Dark brown hair usually means a solid body hit, long white stringy hairs, a paunch or lower body hit, white straight hair would indicate a lower neck shot. Individual scattered hairs which look like they have been cut would indicate a grazing shot, while clumps of hair with skin attached would indicate a solid body hit, the color of the hair indicating where it was located on the deer's body.

The animal's reactions at the shot can sometimes give us clues. Did it flinch, did it change directions or move off in the same direction it was facing when shot, did it move away slowly, (possible kidney or paunch shot) did it break into a fast run, jump up into the air, or kick up its back feet (possible heart shot), hunch up at the shot (possible paunch shot), run erratically with a stumbling gait (solid hit, won't go far), move stiffly and painfully (kidney shot), move away dragging its hind quarters (spinal cord damage in rear section of deer), drop like a rock and then get up and take off (shot close to spinal column, head shot or antler shot). All these reactions can tell us something about where and how seriously the animal was hit. *But even though you notice no obvious indications of a hit it does not mean that you missed!!*

An unalarmed animal will always go down easier than an alarmed deer or a deer already pumped full of adrenalin.

I shot a rutted up buck, when I was a kid, with a direct shot to the neck, which put him down but he refused to die and after about two to three minutes he got a crazed look in his eyes, started moving his feet and actually got up and started running away! A quick shot ended his escape and is what I should have done in the first place.

In an analysis of 493 animals shot at a private hunting club at an average distance of 127 yards, 50% of the deer ran when shot and 25% of these showed no signs of a hit. The deer shot with soft tipped, quicker expanding bullets and heavier calibers, i.e., .257, .270, and other 30 caliber rifles, traveled shorter distances. The average distance traveled with a shoulder shot was 3 yards, heart shot 39 yards, lung shot 50 yards and abdomen 69 yards. All of these shots were taken from hunters in tree stands and predominantly were taken at undisturbed animals.

Try to safely get another shot into the animal. If you press a wounded animal there is more chance for the wound to continue to bleed and cause more internal damage. If you wait, the sign gets older and harder to distinguish, there's the possibility of rain or snow washing away or covering the sign and the possibility of other game animals covering up or interfering with the sign of the animal you're track-ing. If a deer beds for a long time there is a good chance for the wound to clog with fat or congealed blood, which gives you little sign to track from.

I hunt with a rifle and a quick cautious approach to tracking would be my choice! Let your pulse rate drop a little and then follow up the animal as if you were cautiously, still hunt-ing. I have not had enough experience with archery hunt-ing to make my own recommendations on what to do with wounded game but the majority of the articles I've read prefer the "wait and watch" approach, rather than an immediate follow-up.

When you are searching for sign, at the point of impact, and while trailing the animal be careful not to obliterate any sign!!! Travel off to one side of the trail, not directly on it.

As mentioned above you should search for a wounded animal just as you would if you were still hunting. Look for anything out of the ordinary. This is a good time to use you binoculars to scan the cover ahead and around you, for a sight of your trophy.

Note any distinguishing characteristics of the track, such as size, stride, a cut or broken hoof, any information which may help you identify it later.

MOVE SLOWLY

As you move off to the side of the deer's trail mark each piece of evidence you find with surveyors tape, white tis-sue paper or a similar easily visible material and carefully search the area ahead with your binoculars looking for your quarry.

If the animal is not immediately, mortally wounded he will bed off trail, in heavy cover, and will be watching his back trail. Don't just look at eye level, get down on your hands and knees, or better yet squat down, so you aren't disturbing as large an area, and look below standard vegetation height, for sign or actual sight of the wounded animal.

When you are looking for sign, look first for blood on the ground but also look for it on tips of grass, and bushes and scrubs along the sides of the trail, up to a height of 18 to 24". If your shot was a chest shot and you know which side the animal was hit on, concentrate your sight pattern on the opposite side of the animal, i.e., the exit hole side. Heart and lung shot deer especially show blood higher up on vegetation.

Again, be sure and mark every piece of sign you find with surveyors' tape so the location is not lost and also to determine direction of travel. If you have a medical kit back at camp, hydrogen peroxide will help you locate blood or distinguish dried blood from red covered leaves or mud. When hydrogen peroxide comes in contact with blood it will foam and bubble.

A clear heavy blood trail does not have to be marked, but be sure and do not obliterate the trail.

Blood is the best and easiest form of sign to find, but many times there will be little blood. In this case we need to mark every blood location very carefully and look for other sign to tie the blood sign together. Examples of such sign would be upturned leaves, kicked up dirt, overturned rocks and bent or broken grass or scrubs.

Bright red blood found in the hoof print could indicate a leg shot. This is not good. A dragged leg would indicate that there is a rear leg wound and a track where the hoof is at a distinctly different angle from the other tracks would indicate a possible broken or damaged front leg.

Some general rules to follow are: 1. Mortally wounded deer will not necessarily follow trails, and in fact many times will run blindly until they drop dead. They don't travel far, but they can, and are lost because hunters do not pay attention to details and move too quickly. I remember a buck I almost lost, when I was younger, because there was a variety of fresh tracks on the trail he first traveled on, and I was concentrating so hard on the tracks that I walked right past him and couldn't figure out why the blood trail had suddenly disappeared. So I followed the trail back to his original entry point and then got up on a log to get a better perspective. When I did, I saw him piled up about 10 yards off the trail, in a pile of brush. 2. Badly wounded animals tend to head toward water, with still, calm water being the preference and tend to move side hill or down hill. 3. Wounded animals tend to head for familiar security cover or bedding areas. 4. After the initial adrenalin rush and especially if the animal is hit with a shot which is not quickly fatal, a deer will follow existing trails. 5. Wounded game will sometimes double back and then head off at another angle. Look for blood on both sides of the track. 6. Don't use more than two more experienced trackers. 7. If sign is scarce, look at the terrain and travel lanes and make some assumptions on direction of travel based on your marked back trail. 8. If you marked your last area of sign and can't find any additional confirmation, start making increasingly large circles around the last piece of evidence until you find where the deer has gone. 9. If two or more people are tracking, use hand signals, or at the least, talk no louder than a whisper. One person should be doing the tracking while the other person is watching for the animal with gun or bow ready.

A friend and I were doing a two-person still hunt once, when I jumped a nice buck which ran in his direction. When he took the shot the deer was running downhill directly towards him and the bullet broke the deer's shoulder but did not penetrate into the body cavity.

He could have taken another shot, but he was so sure that the deer wouldn't travel far that he did not (Bad Decision #1). I came down to where he was and we started following the sign, which by this time was only a few spots of blood every 30 or 40 yards. I was down on my hands and knees doing the tracking and I told him to watch for the buck with rifle ready, so he could get another shot in.

Unbeknownst to me, after a couple hundred yards of tracking, while I was on my hands and knees, he had put his rifle over his shoulder (Bad decision #2). The buck had bedded down and we jumped him, but my partner was not ready, and did not get the shot. After this, the buck never stopped traveling and we did not catch up with him. A farmer found him a couple of days later laying dead beside one of his irrigation ponds.

SHOT PLACEMENT

Study a diagram of a deer's anatomy to know where the vital organs are located!! (See next page.)

If you're sure about your shooting ability and sight picture, the best shot at close distances would be a shot to the upper bony portion of the deer's neck, at any point from where the neck joins the body up to six or eight inches behind the deer's head.

The traditional bullet behind the shoulder is always a good bet, as it creates a fairly large target and there are several vital organs located in this area, but expect the animal to travel a ways before dropping.

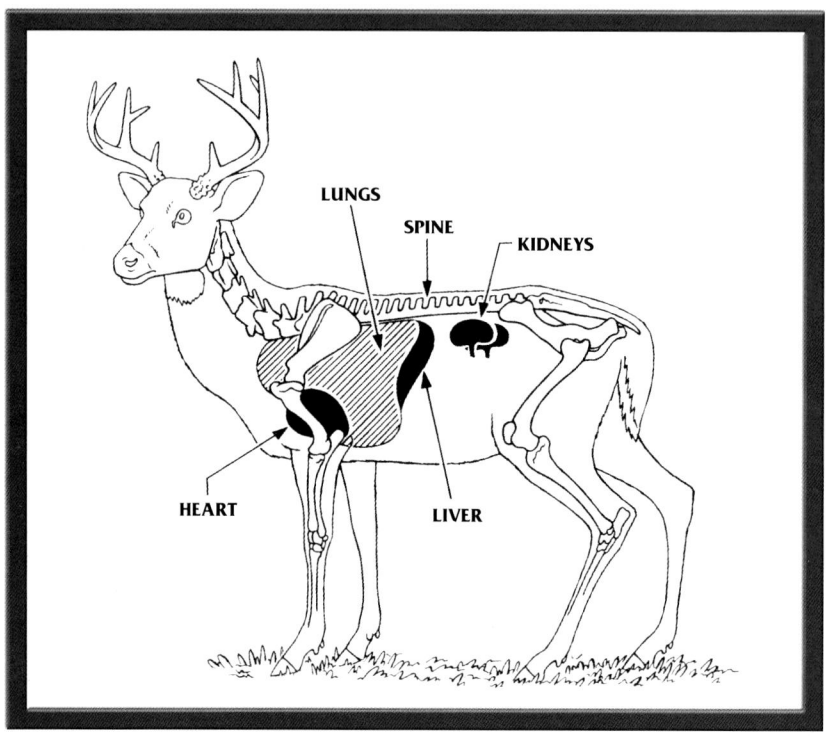

If you're using a heavy solid bullet, a shot directly into the shoulder, on a broadside shot will usually put the animal down, but this shot should not be used with a light caliber gun or light grained or quick expanding bullets. The minimum caliber for this type of shot would be a 30-06 with a slow expanding bullet and the minimum bullet weight would be 180 grains.

I do not recommend rear end shots because there are too many variables involved and too much chance of wounding and losing the animal. If the deer is looking back at you, make the shot at the spot where the neck connects to the body. If all you can see is the rear end don't shoot, wait for a better shot.

When shooting at the neck, if the deer is facing you, aim right at the point where the neck joins the body. If the deer is broadside, aim at the top third of the neck, closer to the vertebrae, and the first 1/3 to 2/3 of the distance above where the neck joins the body. If the deer is below you, aim at the spot between the shoulders where the neck joins the body.

Avoid head shots, or shots at the skinny part of the neck close to the deer's head. There is too much chance of hitting the animal with a glancing head shot or worse yet, a bullet to the jaw. These types of shots, if they are not direct hits, do not hit any vital area and allow the deer to travel for days or months before dying a slow lingering death. Just last year I was asked by a neighbor to try and find a buck whose jaw had been shattered by a poorly placed hunter's bullet. She had jumped the buck when he was bedded by a small pond. Unfortunately, he did not come back and I was unable to find him.

When you're in a tracking situation don't travel more than 30 or 40 yards from your last *confirmed* sign, which in most cases would be blood, because tracks and fresh sign can be, and are made by, other deer. If you haven't found confirming sign turn around and work back to your last marked location, being careful not to disturb the trail. Many times this new line of vision will allow you to see sign you didn't notice from the original direction.

While you're tracking your animal look and listen for other wildlife which might alert you to the location of your quarry.

If you travel a long distance, be sure to keep track of your compass bearings or other landmarks so that when you do find your deer, you can find your way back out! This would also be a great time to use your GPS, if you have one.

In an evening hunting situation, always carry a flashlight, clearly mark where you were shooting from, memorize the deer's location, go back to camp or car and get the largest flashlight you can find, or better yet get a portable lantern and a friend and come back to search for the deer.

Photos showing preferred shot placement

Photo credit: Chuck Bartlett

Photo credit: Chuck Bartlett

Blood will actually be more obvious with the use of a flash-light or especially a lantern. It's also good to write down everything you can remember on a note pad, and it goes without saying, to flag your way out every few feet with florescent surveyors' tape.

I do not recommend long distance evening shots! On evening stands, try to post up as close to where you feel the deer will show, as possible. Any shot over 100 yards is pushing it and 50 yards and under is preferred. This will not only give better visibility, it will give you the opportunity to create a neck shot, versus a behind the shoulder shot. A well placed neck shot will put the animal down immediately and permanently and not set you up for a lengthy and possibly unsuccessful evening tracking job.

When you locate your game, make sure that it is dead before getting too close. Look for glazed eyes or throw a couple of sticks or rocks on it to see if it moves. There is no need to cut a dead deer's neck and it destroys the look of a beautiful animal.

Clean up any blood and take your photos, then begin removing the entrails. I carry disposable plastic gloves for this chore. Once you have found your game and are hauling it out, remove all of your trail and shot placement markers and dispose of your gloves at home.

The final verdict is still out on some of the new "heat sensing", wounded deer finding devices, but if they help people find more wounded game, then I'm personally in favor of them. Also, if you hunt in a state that allows tracking dogs on leashes to locate wounded game, then I would also be in favor of that. Any legal, ethical method that helps locate dead, wounded or suffering game animals quicker and more effectively, I'm in favor of.

Chapter 14

The Ripple Principle

How Unnatural Sound Affects Game and How to Minimize It

*W*e *as hunters do not live in a vacuum! We must realize, that for every action, there is a corresponding reaction in nature!* When we enter the woods, everything we do (or fail to do), affects some part of nature, which in turn affects another and so on down the line. I call this " The Ripple Principle."

Drop a large rock in the water and the ripples steadily get larger and larger and then finally fade away. Drop several small rocks in the water in rapid succession, and the combined effect, though not creating as large an initial effect, will have a much greater ultimate impact. *Careless hunters create their own ripple effect, when they carelessly enter the woods.*

As you drive to your favorite hunting spot, with your radio on, you are beginning the first wave. When you get out of your car, and carelessly slam the door rather than closing it softly, you send out another wave. When you start walking quickly toward your specific destination, you continue to extend the warnings ahead of you.

Game animals have ears, too, and they don`t necessarily prefer your choice of music. The slamming of your car door (an easily identifiable human noise) has alerted any animal within 200 to 500 yards, that there is a human on the prowl. The sound of your hurried footsteps continues the alarm.

The blue jay, camp robber or squirrel you spook, as you boldly march to your destination, the one which loudly scolds you or flies several yards ahead of you, proclaiming your intrusion, has further extended the alarm. Then there's that foolish doe you spooked, the one who ran crashing through the brush for several hundred yards ahead of you!

Well, you weren`t hunting does anyway, were you? I`ve got news for you! Because of the noisy doe, the wary old buck that is the object of your intentions is now long gone or carefully hidden. The series of warnings which you have caused to proceed your arrival have been duly heeded by the local game population, and any mature animal has already silently departed or secured itself in a handy brush patch.

Nature has rolled out "The RED CARPET OF ALARM", ahead of you! The series of noise violations which you have committed or caused to be committed by natures' tattle-tales, has proceeded ahead of you like the series of ripples caused by several rocks thrown in the water. There was not just one loud splash, which faded away and was forgotten, but several continuing small splashes, whose combined effect reached far past your effective visual hunting radius.

These ripples will continue, until you as a hunter break the rhythm and cause the progression to stop. Like the ripple from a single stone, an isolated natural sound violation will run its course and be forgotten, but continued violations will spread out in ever widening circles!

The average hunter is out of place in the woods. He wears unnatural, noisy nylon jackets and stiff pants, which rub and scrape together at every step. Heavy thick soled boots crash noisily to the ground, destroying anything in their path. His arms wave about like the hands on a wind-mill, while his head jerks in every direction. His step is straight and true, with no breaks or variations. The only change in his rhythm is caused by an occasional sneeze or cough, stopping to have a smoke or any of a multitude of typical human idiosyncracies. These unnatural actions alarm small and large animals alike.

Game animals are used to natural occurrences in the woods and are not overly alarmed unless they happen at very close distances or are repeated unnaturally. They have various natural sounds categorized and only respond to those which are alarming. *Sounds which they associate with natural animal movement don't alarm them. Unnatural noises, though, instantly get their attention and they become alert when they hear such suspicious sounds. They then use ALL of their senses to focus and tune in, on the cause of the disturbance.*

It's hard enough trying to combat one of an animal's superior senses, but it's even harder trying to out-maneu-ver all three of them. We must keep the animals at ease and make them feel that what they heard was another undis-turbed game animal, not a human intrusion.

Various types of movements have different effects on game animals, depending on the association attached to the sound. The breaking of twigs and the swishing of branches against soft clothing may alert, but not necessarily alarm. The clanking of loose bullets in a hunter's pocket, the grating of hard-soled boots against a rock, the scraping of branches against a nylon jacket, a cough, the sound of a noisy zipper or the human voice will create instant recognition and alarm. This will cause the animal either to flee or quietly move into the forest undetected. A game animal needs no follow up nor additional sensory identification to respond to these typically human noises.

We as hunters can control what a deer's reactions to our sounds are and how potentially explosive that reaction may be, by taking some simple precautions!

BREAKING THE CHAIN OF EVENTS

Preparation

To control an animal's reaction to our intrusion we need to act and clothe ourselves as they do. Wear soft, quiet, clothing with large broken color variations. Day One Camouflage, Kathy Kelly Designs, Winona Camo System, and now most of the other large clothing manufacturers are producing quiet hunting clothing. Purchase hunting boots with soft soles and learn how to walk quietly and feel your way with your feet. Again there are many manufacturers of quiet foot wear.

Travel with a fluid, uneven gait, pausing often to look and listen! Whenever you move, try to stay in the shadows and screen your outline with natural vegetation.

When you move your arms, raise them as slowly and as unobtrusively as possible. When not in use, keep them tightly against you sides or at waist height in front of you. Paint your face, gun and hands so there are no bright, shiny or unnatural surfaces.

Photo credit: Boyd Iverson

The dominant buck is alert! Note how the three bucks are positioned. Ears, eyes and noses in all directions.

Application

Go with the flow. Enter the woods smoothly and cautiously. If you break a branch, catch the attention of a noisy blue jay or squirrel, or spook an over zealous doe, BREAK THE CYCLE. Do not add more fuel to the fire. Stop immediately, make yourself inconspicuous visually and make no further sounds or movements that might arouse further suspicion. Stay that way for several minutes, maybe even up to half an hour, depending on the habitat and your particular hunting situation. *Game animals have fairly short attention spans and if there are no follow-up sounds to further alert their senses or help them pinpoint the exact location or cause of the disturbance, they will resume their normal behavior.* If, on the other hand, you don't stop, you are sure to create other unnatural noises, which will continue the alarm.

Because of our fast paced existence, the time we spend motionless may seem like eternity. But I have seen deer stand perfectly motionless from five to fifteen minutes and longer when their senses have alerted them to possible danger. Even in their normal activity, they remain motionless for several minutes, as they critically analyze their environment.

If you`ve ever watched an undisturbed mature buck traveling through the woods or approaching a feeding area, you know what I mean. He seemingly glides through the woods, with no quick or harsh movements, cautiously taking a step or two at a time. His eyes are intensely searching out any possible danger, while his ears are cupped and rotate in various directions, like a radar screen, to catch any unfamiliar sounds. He stays in the shadows and keeps his form screened with natural vegetation. He moves again only when he senses that all is well. Many times it is only the uncontrolled flick of an ear or the swish of a tail, that alerts us to his presence.

Save Sounds vs. Alarming Noise

The forest is not naturally silent. In fact, absolute silence can sometimes be more of a warning than sound itself. Have you ever noticed that after you have remained motionless for a few minutes, you start to see and hear the various forest dwellers? The woods seem to suddenly come alive with activity. Actually the animals were there all the time, but your presence had alerted them and caused them to assume protective modes of survival. Once they accepted your presence, they resumed their normal behavior.

A safe sound would be the quiet swishing of fir boughs brushing against the hide of an animal as it casually travels along a trail, pausing often to browse and survey the terrain. An occasional twig is broken, but the normal direction and pattern of movement is natural and non disturbing.

An alarming sound, in contrast, would be unnatural. Examples would be the plodding of heavy footsteps, the breaking of several branches in rapid succession, the sound of another animal as it runs from some unseen enemy and seemingly natural sounds coming from unnatural directions. I'm sure that you can think of many other examples.

Common woods sounds are natural, but noise is not! The type of sound associated with normal animal movement is what distinguishes one animal from another, and animals from man. You should try to imitate these movements, as you travel through the forest. Vary your speed of travel, walk around rather than through obstacles, pause before entering or

Photo credit: Boyd Iverson

He'd heard something! Now he's trying to identify what it is.

crossing openings. If the openings are large don't cross them at all. Don't walk in bright sunlight, Be sure to always screen your human form with natural vegetation.

You can also take advantage of any natural and unnatural disturbances and time your movements to coincide with these noise breakers. A sudden gust of wind rattling through the leaves provides a great opportunity to cover any alarming sounds, as does the sound of a jet or plane flying overhead. One time I even purposely used noise and then silence to shoot a nice buck.

I had been slowly and cautiously still hunting along an old creek bed for a couple of hours with no success. The trail I was walking on abruptly ended at the entry to a large patch of Oregon Grape with no quiet access alternative, so I noisily crashed through the brush and then stood absolutely still. The unnatural noise and then complete silence unnerved a wide antlered buck and he exploded from a patch of vine maple only 40 or 50 yards away. I dropped him as he crossed a small opening.

Any technique which we can use to break the chain of alarm will allow us to be more successful hunters. Learn to follow the normal pattern of woods sounds, use available sound camouflage, and when you make a mistake, stop the impact as soon as you can, by not continuing your distinguishable human noise pattern. Let the environment around you and ahead of you settle down. Begin moving again only when you're sure that awareness of your progress is not being transmitted ahead of you.

One hunter I heard about has mastered several natural animal sounds and will imitate these sounds whenever he makes a sound which he feels might be potentially alarming. He feels that if he does this, game animals will associate the sound with the animal he imitates and will not be alerted to his presence. He usually gets his elk every year so he must have a good idea. Some elk hunters typically use a calf or cow call to disguise their movements.

Everything we do has a direct or indirect affect upon the animals we pursue. No sound or action is isolated or goes unnoticed in the wild. Every unnatural action causes a reaction. Once we realize this and the interrelationship of all of nature's various alarm mechanisms, and use them to our advantage, we will become more sensitive and successful hunters.

Chapter 15

They Only Come Out at Night

Evening Big Buck Survival Tactics

Oregon's blacktail deer season was only four days old as my son and I hunted on BLM land in the McKenzie Unit near Eugene. It was approaching dusk and all of the other hunters had already left the area. We sat on our tree stand admiring the sun slowly sinking in the distance, as the silent woods began to come alive. We could hear the calling of birds, the croaking of frogs and the sound of several squirrels scampering about in the trees. In the stillness we also heard a grouse scratching for food in the forest litter. Then came our favorite sound! The sound of two deer slowly working their way through a dense thicket to our right. We first heard, and then saw a fawn prancing about in the dry leaves, followed seconds later by its more hesitant mother.

Picking up my binoculars for a closer inspection, I was surprised to see that while we were watching the doe and fawn, a large-bodied buck had crept in undetected. He approached the doe and fawn and then angled in our direction. If he continued, he would pass almost underneath us. He did as anticipated and when he was about 15 steps away, I centered the scope's crosshairs on his shoulder and fired. The buck dropped instantly and thus ended my hunting season, only a few hours after it began.

Big bucks need cover, either vegetative cover or the cover of darkness! Many hunters are missing their best opportunity for bagging a large buck because of their natural inclination to be

Photo credit: Boyd Iverson

My son Jordan with a late evening buck we took together. B & C score is 94 after deduction of 22 points for non-symmetry.

"walking" rather than "waiting", during the last few precious minutes of legal hunting light!

A study done in 1997 by the Oregon Department of Fish and Game, using trial timers with cameras showed that 83% of the bucks were photographed between 10:00 PM and 5:00 AM, while 56% of the does and fawns were photographed during this same time and only 17% of the bucks traveled during the day light hours of between 7:00 AM and 7:00 PM.

Hunters, possibly because of childhood fears of the "unknown", or scary stories told around dimly-lit campfires, typically plan their agendas so they reach camp or car a "safe" time before dark. In doing this they dramatically diminish their chances for success.

Numerous telemetric studies have shown that, in heavily hunted habitat, large bucks do not get up from their beds to feed until the last few minutes of available light. By this time most hunters have already left or are noisily and hastily departing the woods.

If you want to shoot mature bucks in the habitat typical of most of western Oregon's recreational areas, you need to be prepared to hunt these last excitement-filled minutes.

I have taken several trophy bucks in this manner, a couple of which have made the Boone and Crockett Record Book. During this time I have seen only one other hunter in the woods except those which I passed as they were leaving to get out before dark and one set of hunters I found who were lost. Mature bucks are aware of this hunter migration and consider this an evening "safe" zone.

The oldest buck which I've taken, since I've started scientifically determining the actual age of the animals, is 9 years, and the average age of the bucks which I've taken, while hunting during this time, is a little over eight years.

All of these bucks have "been around the block." These are bucks, who live on public land and have survived several hunting seasons, in intensely hunted locations. They've learned how to survive!

The age of all these bucks was determined by tooth analysis, where a thin cross-section of the tooth is cut out and then a high power microscope is used to count the growth rings in the tooth, the same way they determine the age of a tree.

When most hunters are considering hiking out of the woods, a smart hunter should be heading in! He should carry all of the essentials needed to find his way back out of the woods after dark as well as the ever present emergency kit, fitted into a small fanny pack. My kit contains spare flashlight batteries and compass, a butane lighter, magnesium striker, dry wood shavings, spare knife, 100 feet of nylon twine, light plastic tarp, space tube, and a couple of chocolate candy bars. *Like your American Express Card, "you shouldn't leave home without it"!*

Once my flashlight accidently turned on in my fanny pack and I would have had to spend the night in the woods had it not been for a hunting acquaintance who just happened to be in the area, saw my vehicle, and came looking for me.

A simple way to keep this from happening is to turn the batteries around with opposite polarities until you are ready to use them, or enlist the help of that ever ready duct tape and tape the on-off switch so that it does not come on until you want it to. As a back up I now also carry a very small but bright,Photon Micro-light with a lithium battery

On another occasion, a friend and I lost our sense of direction on a foggy, windy, rainy evening and became disoriented. We spent over an hour going around in circles. I was soaked and nearing hypothermia before we finally found our way out. All this time we were in familiar hunting territory and only about 300 yards from an old logging road. If I had been carrying my emergency kit I could have easily gotten out or at the least been very comfortable waiting out the storm.

At this time of day, with the limited vision afforded us as humans, it is a time to be watching, not walking! It is crucial that you become situated a half-hour to an hour before you expect to see your quarry appear. This allows the wood's creatures to settle down before the appointed hour.

You will notice that when you first establish your stand that there will be no natural animal sounds. But after 10 or 15 minutes your intrusion is forgotten and nature resumes her normal undisturbed activity patterns. This is crucial, because a smart old buck which approaches a feeding area will listen for these signs of activity to determine if the coast is clear. If his senses warn him that something is wrong he will slip back into his protective cover and you will never even know he was near.

Photo credit: Chuck Bartlett

A big, old buck moving out of heavy cover at dusk!

You should establish your stand between a common bedding and feeding location, taking wind direction and trail travel patterns into consideration. It's best to use an elevated tree stand, but the second best choice is a well camouflaged ground blind with as much natural vegetation as possible, to conceal your human form and cover possible body movement. You can also carry a large piece of camouflage cloth with ties on the end, which can be draped over your body, or tied in front of you. Be sure and always rest your back against a tree or have some other vegetation behind you to break up your human silhouette and give you a solid support for your back. Once you are situated, clear away any branches, dry leaves, twigs or similar items which could make noise when you raise your rifle or bow to shoot, or when you need to check out an approaching animal with your binoculars.

If you are hunting in heavily wooded habitat, you may wish to position your stand near, or at the edge of the feeding zone, to take advantage of all available light. Make yourself comfortable, and most importantly, don't move!

With our inferior eyesight, especially in dim light situations, the animal we hunt has many advantages. Our only advantage is that we know what our weak points are and how to overcome them. Even our eyes can pinpoint motion as long as we have time to analyze it. Also with the aid of the superior optics now available, we can squeeze out a few more minutes of shooting time or better view what we think we see in the evening shadows.

Many times though, even with the best of optics and the best of plans, we come up losers. I remember two distinct encounters where this occurred. I had been watching an opening close to a major feeding location when a small fork-horn buck came out, close to dusk. He fed for a few minutes in the diminishing light and then when it became too dark to distinguish detail, two very large-bodied bucks came out of the woods on either side of him. These two bucks fought for several minutes, but even though I was only 40 yards away and could clearly see them fight and hear the sound of their heavy antlers smashing together, I was unable to distinguish antler size and so I did not fire.

Another time, I was on a stand when several does and small bucks started coming to feed 20 to 30 minutes before dusk. Deer continued to arrive until there were a total of 14 deer within 10 to 30 yards of my stand. Finally, when it was too late to determine antler size, two large bucks came out of the woods near my stand and began to feed. Though they were only a few yards away they were safe, because the mantle of darkness protected them.

In several studies done by attaching radio collars to wild deer, it has been shown that deer in general, and large mature bucks in particular, become more nocturnal with age and with increased hunting pressure.

When we stop seeing deer in their normal locations we usually assume that they have departed the area. But what these studies have shown is that, more often than not, the deer have not left, but have simply buried themselves in the thickest brush patch or the most inaccessible or least obvious cover, they can find. Here, they remain safe and secure all day and only venture forth for food when darkness descends. They even establish different feeding habits and spend most of their time in locations which are more protected and provide all of their physical and security needs. These studies show clearly that the deer have not left, they have simply adjusted their routine to fit the circumstance.

To grow a trophy-sized set of antlers, a buck typically needs to have survived at least four or five hunting seasons. By then he is a veteran, has his routine down, and knows his home territory extremely well. If a hunter is going to outsmart a wise old buck, he needs to catch him when he is most vulnerable. The best time to do this is that magical few moments when the sun is rising in the morning and when the sun is setting in the evening, and the deer are traveling to reach their favorite bedding or feeding spot. At this time, a smart hunter should be comfortably seated, watching his favorite trail in anticipation of catching a big old buck unawares. Let the deer make the first wrong move!

I remember the first large late-evening blacktail I purposely outfoxed. I had been analyzing a tract of land for over a year and had located a site that I felt would be good for an evening stand. I positioned myself well before prime time and settled down to wait and watch. Having made sure that my human form was adequately screened, both front and rear, I needed only to move my eyes to survey the specific set of trails I felt the deer would travel on.

About 15 minutes before dusk several does and one small buck showed up and I watched them feed contentedly. Eventually, a new deer began to approach my hiding place. This animal was much larger than any of the previous deer and proceeded very slowly and cautiously toward the feeding area, stopping every two or three steps to survey his domain. Just as he was ready to enter the opening, he stopped for one last look, his head obscured by branches. Even with binoculars the vegetation kept me from telling how large his antlers were.

At last he took a couple more steps and twisted his neck to investigate a sound or scent behind him. With this new perspective I detected a high, wide set of antlers. That was good enough for me. I slowly raised my rifle and fired!

But my shot had no effect! With trembling fingers I quickly put another round in the chamber and fired again.

At my second shot the deer vanished. I jumped up excitedly, ran to where the deer had been standing and found my trophy lying dead, killed instantly with a shot to the neck.

Upon further inspection I found where my first bullet had been deflected by one of the many branches hanging down in front of his neck.

An especially good time to use this technique is when there is a setting sun and a rising moon which occur at about the same time. This situation only happens two or three times during the fall hunting season, so make sure you mark them on your calendars.

In this situation, deer start getting up to proceed to their feeding locations, as the sun starts to go down. But with the moon beginning to rise at the same time or within a few minutes of the setting sun, instead of it continuing to get darker, the dusk lingers or it can actually get slightly lighter. This allows us a few, very valuable, minutes of additional visibility. I have seen the largest number of bucks in these type of sun-moon phases.

Some of the most enjoyable times I have experienced have been right at, or after dusk. A magical stillness comes over the woods, and on many a moonlit night I have watched deer literally feed and play underneath my stand. One evening I had three bucks "trap" me in my stand for almost two hours. I had to stay in my stand so as not to spook them and betray my observation post. I even threw small branches near them to try to get them to leave, but instead of leaving, one of the bucks walked over and began to eat the lichen that was on the branch. As a last resort I pointed my flashlight in their eyes and they finally left.

If you're hunting in a new region and are unsure about your way, you should flag your trail with surveyors' tape, put small notches in the bark of specific trees, or even attach

All good things come to those who wait!

The bucks on this and the next page were all taken from late evening stands.

Photo credit: Jerry Gowins, Jr.

Photo credit: Boyd Iverson

reflective tape to appropriate locations. I prefer surveyors' tape since it is easily removed when I have memorized natural night time landmarks. Permanent blaze marks can damage trees and lead other hunters to your special spot.

To be a successful evening hunter you need to hunt a mile or two from roads and people. A location this far away does not receive the heavy hunting pressure typical of sections closer to traveled roads. Most hunters will not travel this far from the road, and the ones who do will start heading back to the car or camp a half hour to an hour before dark. As mentioned before, the deer are aware of this evening exodus.

It is important that the area you intend to hunt remain undisturbed because, as studies show, if there is continued activity caused by noisy hunters, the cautious older bucks will come out even later than they normally do.

Mature bucks know their home territory intimately and they, like humans, learn shortcuts to special areas and know when it's safe to feed at these eating places. They also locate bedding sites where they are least disturbed and learn to feed in adjacent habitat at a time when they are most secure. You, as an evening hunter, can locate these prime sites and position yourself accordingly.

I hunt by what I call the "Rule of 45." In the early morning or the late evening, when deer are most active and when our eyesight is most ineffective, I sit, for at least the first 45 minutes in the morning and the last 45 minutes in the evening. By following this simple rule you will see your success rate increase dramatically!

As mentioned previously, be sure that you are watching, not walking during these low light situations, when unaided human eyesight is no match for a game animal's natural vision. If we are moving, deer easily spot us and are gone long before we even know they were anywhere around. On the other hand, if we are immobile, we can take advantage of modern magnified optics and our eye's ability to detect motion, even in low light situations, and change the odds.

If a hunter combines his use of stand hunting with his knowledge of the habits and habitat of his quarry, removes his fear of the dark, and situates himself to watch the appropriate trails or feeding locations in late evening, his success will increase dramatically. *Let other hunters walk out of the woods at dusk and let a big buck walk into your sights, by hunting during this special time!*

Chapter 16

Winds of Change

Some New Ideas on How Deer Use Wind Direction

It's time that we as hunters, rethink out beliefs on deer and their responses to wind direction. Con*trary to what we have read and been told for countless years, deer DO NOT always travel, bed, or feed with the wind in their face!*

Does this sound like heresy or an insult to motherhood and apple pie? Well, so be it! For years, hunters have accepted, without question, the statement that, "game animals always travel and feed with the wind in their face". But I have found that this isn't always true! In fact just the opposite is true!! *In certain situations, deer purposely position themselves so that the wind is at their backs or behind them!*

I originally observed this habit in the early 80's, but felt that what I noted were just isolated incidents. It was only after studying my hunting notes, taken while watching an evening feeding location for a period of five years, where I recorded deer activity under varying wind and weather conditions, that I finally realized that there was a pattern to the deer's movement, but that pattern was not what I had always read and been told.

The deer in my area of observation traveled from a hillside bedding area and entered their first feeding area, located on a small bench, from one of three locations, depending on wind direction. *On all of these trails, contrary to common thought, the deer would enter their feeding location with the wind at their backs, not in their faces.*

When the wind was blowing in such a way that they could not approach the feeding area with the wind *at their backs*, they would feed elsewhere. *At no time* did they move into the feeding area with the wind in their face.

Now after observing this "isolated incident" several hundred times, I have accepted it as the rule rather than the exception. By using this newly gained knowledge and positioning myself accordingly, I have taken numerous large bucks. If I had continued to believe what I had always read and been told, about how deer travel with the wind in their face, these bucks would still be roaming the woods.

My research has shown that in the evening, deer will enter a primary feeding area with the wind at their backs rather than in their faces. As they approach their chosen area the deer depend on their eyes and ears to locate danger in front of them and they depend on their noses and the wind to protect their flank.

My findings are based on over 300 plus sightings of deer during 12 years of researching the same general area under various wind and weather conditions. I have backtracked all trails and have recorded the wind and weather conditions during each deer sighting. *At no time have deer approached this feeding area or several other feeding locations, which I have also researched, with the wind in their faces!*

The deer enter the feeding areas with the wind at their backs and position themselves in such a way that the wind will continue to be at their backs while feeding. They also move out of this initial feeding location with the wind behind them.

Although this habit is contrary to popular teaching, in analyzing the situation from a deer's perspective, this survival technique makes perfect sense. Predators such as cougars, bob-cats, coyotes and wolves are a deer's main enemy and therefore deer have developed habits and instincts to protect themselves from these natural enemies.

Contrary to what many Hollywood movies have shown, predators normally do not wait in ambush, but rather stalk about continually, on game trails and through bedding locations, until they locate a fresh scent and then track their prey by its scent trail. For this reason a deer's back trail and its bedding location are very vulnerable positions. But a deer is especially vulnerable while it is feeding since its eyesight and its sense of hearing are hindered.

Given that a deer's sense of smell is its most infallible sense, their instincts teach them to position themselves so that this sense is working best while their other senses are limited. Therefore *while feeding and while bedded, deer position themselves so that the area most immediately behind them is covered by the prevailing wind.*

While traveling from a bedding to a feeding location a deer will spend the greatest amount of effort to protect this vulnerability. This is why the dominant buck, since he is the biggest and strongest, will bring up the rear, when he is traveling with a group of deer.

Since a deer's vision is limited when feeding and its hearing is also adversely affected by the noise it makes while engaged in this activity, its sense of smell is its first and also its most infallible line of defense. This is why a deer will suddenly pop up its head every few seconds, and why it will stop feeding and just listen as it rotates its radar-like ears around, to catch any stray suspicious sounds. Notice how your hearing is affected while you're chewing. This is why a deer's nose becomes its eyes and ears while in these vulnerable positions.

If a deer hears an unidentifiable sound it will usually wait for further confirmation, if it sees something suspicious it will investigate further, but if it smells an unfamiliar or unnatural odor it reacts immediately and needs no further warning. *Their sense of smell is the single most effective and immediate alarm mechanism that a game animal possesses.*

In a deer's daily life cycle, it eats, it sleeps, and it travels between these two life functions. As it travels it uses wind currents for an alarm system.

In the morning a deer will travel from its evening feeding or bedding areas to its chosen daytime bedding location, either with the wind in its face or slightly cross ways to its direction of travel. This will warn it of any predators which might be ahead of it, as it approaches its preferred bedding location.

Once the deer tests the wind and feels comfortable that its proposed bedding spot is secure, it will either move directly to the location or it will move off trail, make a small partial loop, away and usually uphill from the trail and then will loop back towards its back trail, or it will move past the preferred bedding spot and then make a small loop back into this cover, so that the prevailing wind will always be behind the deer when it beds. In this manner the prevailing wind will once again warn it of immediate danger from behind, while its eyes can watch approaching trails and its ears can listen for potential danger. *This means that normally a buck will NOT BE facing the direction of the prevailing wind, when he is bedded, and he will be watching and be bedded above his initial approach trails.* Think about what this means to you when you are still hunting through prospective cover.

Later in the morning when the temperature increases and the thermal air currents begin to move uphill, the deer's back trail scent, closest to where it is bedded, is not as fresh and therefore the deer's bedding location is not as exposed. At this time its eyes and ears will get assistance from the rising air currents and warn it of any intruders which have picked up its old scent trail and are trying to sneak up on it from below. At this time the deer may even get up and change its bedding location in regard to changed wind direction or thermals and temperature.

Telemetric studies have shown that even though a deer spends a majority of its time bedded, approximately 70% in

Photo credit: Chuck Bartlett

Wind and cover behind and visibility to backtrail!

undisturbed situations, it will only stay bedded in one location for a maximum of about three hours.

In the early evening when a buck again thinks of food, he will arise from his bed, secure that all is safe below and then will proceed to the chosen food source. Since he may have bedded in the same general area for most of the day or at the least, for the last few hours, instinct tells him that he has left a strong scent trail which can be easily picked up and followed by predators.

At this time the thermals are beginning to reverse directions and are starting to move downhill with the cooling evening air. As the deer moves downhill it will move with the wind and will depend primarily on its eyes to guard its downhill route. As it nears its chosen feeding area the deer will move even slower and more cautiously and will continue to search out danger with its eyes and ears and will position itself so that once it begins feeding its back-trail will be covered with the prevailing wind.

While eating, a deer will pop its head up periodically to visually survey the surrounding area which is not protected by its sense of smell and it will rotate its ears in various directions to pick up any unusual or alarming sounds. *But in my observations it's always the deer's nose which first alerts it to another animal's approach from its back trail!*

I can always tell when another deer or animal is approaching from behind because the feeding deer will pop up its head and focus its attention on its back trail anywhere from two to five minutes before the next deer or animal arrives. Since visibility is very limited in this area and there are several well-worn, quiet deer trails entering the feeding location, the deer could only know about the new animal's potential arrival by its sense of smell.

I was watching a large buck one year while he was feeding, when suddenly he picked up his head, turned and

Photo credit: Boyd Iverson

Photo of one of the bears which spooked the buck I was watching.

looked back toward his back trail and then quickly bolted out of the opening.

It was during the rut, and I had seen similar action from other smaller bucks when the dominant buck was approaching. I was prepared to see a monster buck move out of the brush and into my sights, but instead about a minute later, two twin black bears burst out of the woods and followed the buck's scent out of the opening. These two bears had picked up the bucks trail scent and had fig-ured that they had an easy meal, but the bucks positioning of the wind and his keen sense of smell saved his life.

I was disappointed that it wasn't the dominant buck which I had expected, but the bears were fun to watch and it again clearly indicated how important wind direction is in warning deer of approaching danger.

When the wind is such that the deer cannot leave their bedding area and arrive at my observation locations, using the wind as their rear guard, they don't show! I haven't found out yet where they go, but I'm sure that their alternative feeding area is situated in such a way that they can use the wind as their rear alarm system.

We as successful hunters and animal observers, need to throw out the rule that tells us that deer always travel, bed or feed with the wind in their face. It's not so, and given the information about instinct and survival, it doesn't even make "scents". (Pardon the pun.)

When deer are moving to their chosen bedding area in the morning, they travel with the wind in their face, or cross wise to the wind. But I have found, at least in the brush-filled habitat where I hunt and in situations where the deer are bedded on hillsides and then travel downhill a relatively short distance to their primary evening feeding areas, there is no doubt in my mind that the deer prefer the wind at their backs.

During the 1995 deer season I was checking out a new hunting spot and I located an area with numerous indistinct trails with lots of fresh tracks leading from some heavier cover to a six or eight year old clear cut.

I knew that any self-respecting old buck would not enter the clear cut until well after dark, but I figured that if I positioned myself 300 to 400 yards from the clearing in the most open area in the woods that I could find (I needed the openness to capture what little light might be available once the sun started setting) that I might be able to intercept a cautious old buck as he was approaching the over grown clear cut for his evening meal.

I set up for the evening, positioned my ground stand close to, and downwind of the trails where I believed the deer would be traveling and waited.

I didn't have long to wait! Shortly after the sun had slowly settled into the tree tops a large old buck crept cautiously down one of the trails I was watching. As he paused, partially screened by a small fir tree, at a distance of 18 steps, I solved all of his future food desires. To date this is the largest, true 3 point, ie., three points and no eyeguards, that I have taken. He was tooth aged at seven and a half years old. *I was able to outsmart this mature buck only because of my knowledge of how deer move with the wind!*

If you analyze the wind direction in your favorite hunting spots on the basis of the above observations, you will have an added trick to put in your hunting possibilities bag. This knowledge will help you put venison on the table and racks on the wall when others go without. *Learn to think like a deer and you may change some of your other pre-conceived hunting ideas!*

Photo credit: Boyd Iverson

My largest true 3 x 3 with no eyegaurds. 7.5 years old. Antlers are narrow but very high and very symmetrical. Width is impressive but over rated as far as scoring is concerned. Net B & C score is 110.

Chapter 17

Moon Madness

Ideas About How the Moon May Affect Your Hunt

Aperson would have to be "mad" to say that he knows exactly what deer will do in relation to the moon's appearances and disappearances since there are such a wide set of variables that affect a deer's actions more than just the phases of the moon. Time of year, temperature, rising or lowering barometer, snow, rain, wind conditions, cloud cover, hunting pressure all can, and do, have a greater or over-riding affect than any possible moon effects.

But nonetheless, with all this said, there seems to be some general principles which can help us choose which

Photo credit: Chuck Bartlett

days would be our most effective hunting days in relation to the various moon phases, all other things being equal.

Over time there have been many theories proposed about how good hunting is or is not under various moon conditions. Recently there has been a lot of press devoted to various moon theories.

All of this information is very interesting and leads to some of the same general conclusions reached by the various theories.

First, when we talk about various moon phases, we need to define what we are talking about, so here are the definitions and explanations. We will start the cycle with a new moon or dark moon, i.e., the time when we see no moon. The next phase is called a 1/4 moon which is when the moon is overhead. This actually looks like a 1/2 moon visually. The next phase is the full moon. Then there is the 3/4 moon or moon under foot, which again looks like a 1/2 moon visually. Then there is the new or dark moon to again end the cycle. The first 1/4 moon (moon overhead) happens at 7.5 days, a full moon happens at around 14.8 days, the next 3/4 moon (moon underfoot) happens at 22 1/2 days and then a new moon occurs again at 29.5 days.

The most important thing, according to these studies, is when the moon peaks, either above or below where we are, since they believe that deer feed in relation to this gravitational pull and react in relation to increasing and decreasing amounts of light.

Here are some general principles or theories which may help you pick the best times to hunt in relation to the location of the moon.

1. More deer are taken on days following dark evenings and the fewest following a full moon, unless it is a rising moon in the evening which starts its ascent a little bit before, or about the same time as the setting sun. On the day after a dark or quarter moon peak activity occurs from 6:00 A.M. to 9:00 A.M. On the day after a full moon deer normally come out later in the day and the peak activity is from 3:00 P.M. until 9:00 P.M. but they will have a short mid-day feeding movement.

During a full moon in November, bucks move a lot during the middle of the day. Deer will bed earlier on the days following a full moon, especially if the weather is hot. Most deer are taken during the week before the full moon and the week after the full moon.

2. As mentioned before, if you have a late afternoon moon (the fuller the better) rising time, which starts a half hour before the suns sets or just as the sun sets this is an excellent time to be on a stand in the evening, watching a feeding location or trails between bedding areas and feeding areas.

Deer start moving to their evening rituals as the sun starts to set and the sky darkens, but then instead of getting darker, with the earlier rising moon, it actually becomes lighter for a period of time and this fools the deer's time schedule.

I have seen the largest number of deer on evening stands with this situation.

3. When the new moon or full moon peaks overhead or under foot at 10:30 A.M. to 2:30 P.M. the deer will only move a few yards to a few hundred yards to feed during this time and will feed for a short period of time. This type of moon happens about 2/3's of the lunar cycle.

The best hunting opportunities exist around sunrise and sunset when the 1/4 or 3/4 moon peaks either over head or under foot at these times. This happens the other 1/3 of the lunar cycle.

4. The full moon in late October or November, called the "Hunters' Moon", which is the 2 nd. full moon after the fall equinox on September 21st may trigger the estrous cycles for does north of the 40th latitude. Northern California, Washington and Oregon are all north of the 40th. latitude.

For this rut activity to be most effective, the weather needs to be cold and clear, there needs to be light hunting

Photo credit: Chuck Bartlett

Buck moving near security cover during mid-day.

Photo credit: Chuck Bartlett

This buck is scent checking a trail during mid-day.

pressure, you must have the right age groups in your deer herds, and the buck to doe ratio needs to be two to three does per buck.

Bucks will become active a few days before this full moon, and up until six or seven days after the full moon, then the does will enter estrous and the prime breeding will occur as the moon hits its dark phase. When the moon is full, hunt close to bedding areas and travel routes between bedding and security cover. There will be a lot of mid-day "seeking" activity during this time.

If you believe in using doe in heat scents now would be the time to use them. This should also be the best time to rattle. But once the breeding starts, buck activity drops. Now concentrate your time hunting downwind of known bedding locations. Does will tend to be more active during this time and bucks less active.

Does will stay in estrous for 24 hours and in a balanced herd, sixty to eighty percent of the does are bred during this first cycle. The remaining does which have not been bred will re-cycle in 25 to 29 days.

You can locate the moon rise and moon set tables and the various moon phases in the various outdoor magazines and some of the hunting and fishing calendars. Also, most GPS units can tell you moon rising and moon setting dates.

I have read numerous articles to get some of these general principles, but the results and the time of deer sightings do vary between the different professional studies and individual hunter's records of their long term observations.

The reasons for these differences can relate to personal hunting style and the location in the habitat where the hunter spent his time (i.e., trail watcher, still hunter, stand hunter, hunting security cover or bedding cover versus trails between feeding and bedding and bedding and feeding), states hunted in, weather and temperature during the moon phases, doe to buck ratios or the number of deer in the area, type of habitat hunted and I'm sure several other variables I haven't thought of yet. But, it is an interesting study with some interesting assumptions which should be of benefit to the hunter.

The information above was obtained from my own observations, articles by Charles J. Alsheimer, studies by Wayne LaRoche, Doctor Grant R. Woods, and Greg Koch, and a book written by Jeff Murray entitled "Moon Struck" and published by Fool Moon Press, 5702 Fish Lake Dam, Duluth, MN 55803. (1-800-449-6645) Jeff Murray also produces a moon dial guide each year, which tells when and where he feels the best hunting will take place in relation to the location of the moon.

Chapter 18

Which Way Did We Go?

General GPS info
by Mark Armstrong

GPS UNITS AND HOW THEY WORK

GPS units receive signals from 27 satellites, managed by the Department of Defence, which orbit in outer space. Each GPS unit uses information transmitted from these satellites to determine a precise location on the ground, to locate where you are, where you've been or where you want to go. To compute an accurate location or speed of travel, the GPS unit needs to lock onto at least three satellites. If you want to compute height or elevation the GPS unit needs to lock on to at least four satellites.

GPS units work any where in the world, 24 hours a day. Weather does not affect GPS transmission, but tall forested areas can and do. In forested areas the quality of the GPS unit and its antennae and the ability of the unit to lock on to more than one satellite at a time become critical, for the operation and accuracy of the unit.

NAVIGATING WITH GPS

All GPS hand held receivers designed for outdoor use perform the same type of navigation with some variations and different knobs, buttons, and features.

For basic outdoor situations you should set your unit to display Latitude and Longitude in degrees, minutes, and seconds or degrees and decimal minutes.

Carry your GPS unit with you as you travel, hike or go on vacations, to become familiar with how it works. Don't depend on it in potentially dangerous or important situations until you know how and why it functions and operates.

When you reach camp turn on your unit and fix and store your position with an easily remembered name in the GPS library. For our illustration we'll use "camp". Then go hunting or hiking. When you're ready to return to camp turn your unit back on and wait until your new position has been located, then pick the "Go To", "From A to B" or similar menu (each GPS unit has its own name for this) and pick "camp" out of the library. An azimuth and a distance will be displayed. Take out your compass and dial in your azimuth back to camp, make a mental note of the distance to camp and then turn your GPS unit off, to save the batteries.

It's not a bad idea to carry a small note pad and pencil along with you to record information for later use and an extra set of batteries, would also be a cheap form of insurance.

STORING AND NAMING LOCATIONS

The following discussion assumes that the user is familiar with and knows how to use a compass. Most GPS receivers allow storage of 250 or more locations. These positions can be named so that you can remember where they are.

If you hunt in a variety of locations it becomes important to learn how to become creative with names. Obviously four or five locations all named "camp" will not get you to where you want to go. You will want to develop a naming system that is simple, but easy to remember.

While hunting in Alaska for Caribou, I was in an area with 10 or more lakes and I stored the locations of these lakes so I could head to the one I wanted and set a route for each days hunt.

It was a struggle to come up with unique names that I could remember. Our bush pilot also had a GPS in his plane, and we set up the coordinates for the larger lakes so that he could land and pick up the meat when we got our caribou.

When you're using your GPS, always be careful not to delete any locations while in the field, unless you are absolutely sure you won't need them. If you're miles from camp and accidently delete your "camp" coordinate from your library, your GPS unit won't do you any good.

If you have very important locations which you want to remember, its a good idea to write the latitude and longitude and the name of the site in your notebook. If your batteries go dead or your memory is deleted in some manner you will always be able to re-enter the information once your unit is up and running.I would say that a good rule of thumb to follow, is to never erase information while in the field or camp! Do your erasing of information, if needed, once you're home.

SELECTIVE AVAILABILITY

All GPS receivers that are not differentially corrected are subject to the effects of the Department of Defence adjustments to the satellite's position and internal clocks and ephemeris. These adjustments are what can be loosely termed selective availability. The result of these adjustments is that the exact location of your position can be off by up to 320 to 350 feet.

But for a point of information, the U.S. Coast Guard broadcasts corrections for Selective Availability and if you can get these corrections you will know exactly how far off your unit is, at any given time, since these adjustments are made on a random continuing basis.

So how accurate are the various GPS units? When selective availability is off, units should be within 30 to 60 feet, and when it's on, as mentioned before, within 320 to 350 feet. If you need better than 15 to 20 foot accuracy then you need to use DGPS differential correction, but usually if you locate a distinctive landmark near your location or flag the area near your desired location, the normal accuracy level is all you need. Some of the newer units will indicate when selective availability is functioning and when it isn't.

GPS, TOPOGRAPHICAL MAPS AND TREES

Some of the GPS units have topographical maps stored in their memory, plus you can purchase U.S.G.S. 7.5' maps from several companies and there are several new computer programs which allow you to access and print topographical maps from the various states. There are also several new books and computer programs which will give you specific coordinate locations for some, if not all, of the states.

I have been in forests of every kind and I have never had to move more than 100 feet or so to get the necessary three satellite connections, even in old growth forests, where trees are 200 plus feet tall.

The trick is to understand that satellites are traveling at 6000 miles per hour and transmitting continually, and technically, although they are supposed to be all around you they are more to the south than the north. The satellites that are low to the horizon have to pass through more trees than the ones straight above you. So, if you are patient and willing to move around a little you can generally get a fix. The newer receivers which have eight or more parallel channels are faster and can take advantage of signals coming between trees. So if you are in a heavily treed environment, try it first at your first choice of positions, but if that location does not work, move around some and try to find a more open area or point the GPS unit in a different direction.

APPLICATION: By Boyd Iverson

Mark has given you some technical and "how-to" information and I am going to discuss some of the many scenarios where the knowledge of how to correctly use a GPS unit can be beneficial or even life saving. I am currently not well versed in their use, since I have a personal aversion to computers but I have purchased a GPS unit and I am trying to overcome my mental blocks.

Situations where the knowledge of how to use a GPS unit would be beneficial: 1. Set up GPS coordinates for your stand or tree stand locations so you can find them easily in the dark. 2. Set up GPS location of particular roads you need to find to access your chosen hunting area so you can locate them easily in the dark. 3. Set up GPS coordinates for camp or car so you can find it in the dark. 4. Set up GPS coordinates to mark the location of where you left your buck at night, or where you quit trailing a wounded animal. 5.Set up GPS coordinates on distinct land marks as you still hunt during the day so that you can find your way back, not only in daylight, but also after dark or in the case of a bad storm. 6. Study the topographical map and aerial photo of any new area you intend to hunt and pick likely locations then input the coordinates of these locations into your GPS unit, so that you can, with the use of your compass and GPS unit, go directly to these locations, i.e. a bench in steep country, an opening in the woods, a good looking finger ridge, etc. 7. Set up GPS coordinates which will tell you whether you are on private property or government or state property while hunting, to make sure that you have the right to hunt where you are hunting. 8. Set up GPS coordinates so you can return to where you have taken a deer in previous years or so you can return to a particularly good looking deer trail, vantage point, clearing or similar situation. 9. Set up GPS coordinates on various roads which surround or access the area you plan to hunt so that when you get game or need to get out, you can locate the closest or easiest route.

The computer age is upon us and we all need to treat these new products as friends and use them to our benefit!

Chapter 19

Eyes to the Future

How We Can Protect the Future of Hunting

First, let me say that I am proud to be a hunter and sportsman and I make no apologies for my love of the outdoors, because no apologies are needed, but we all need to learn to be sensitive to those in the community who do not hunt.

We should take good, blood free, tongue in mouth photos of our trophies. We shouldn't mount elk or deer heads on the front of our rigs, strap them to the tops of our cars or leave deer heads hanging out of the rear of our trunks. *In short, we should respect others as well as the game we hunt!*

Photo credit: Boyd Iverson

Authors son on a father and son deer hunt.

I'm not saying not to be proud of the fact that you're a hunter and not to be proud of the game which you have taken, but choose the appropriate location to do your bragging.

We as sportsmen and sportswomen need to get our act together and get involved in local, state or national groups which promote wildlife and good sportsmanship. We need to police our own ranks and if we see other "hunters" who are violating game laws or acting unethically we should report them to the appropriate law enforcement agencies. Respect private property rights. Always ask permission to hunt on private property and leave camp cleaner and better than you found it.

Game enforcement officers are too few, with too much land to look after, and they need our assistance. Almost every state now has a 1-800 number you can call to report game violations anonymously and most states also have rewards for such reports. The Oregon Hunters' Association, with financial assistance from Leupold and Stevens, has sponsored the Turn In a Poacher program in conjunction with the Oregon State Police. The number for the Oregon program is 1-800-452-7888.

I would hope that the promise of payment wouldn't be the main reason that we turn in poachers and game violators, but many times money talks and if that's what it takes, then it's worth the cost.

If you hear about judges who aren't afraid to levy fines for game violations, write them letters to say that you approve. Or if you find judges who feel that game violations are unimportant, write and let them know that you disagree and that you vote!

We also need to unite and not quibble about what type of weapon we use. The animal, not the weapon, should be our first and final concern.

Spend some time and take your children or other youngsters into the woods to teach them sportsmanship and the love and appreciation of God's creation. The Bible tells us to "Raise up a child in the way he should go and when he grows up he will not depart from it."

Magazines, books, videos, and movies can't do it. We need to spend time with our children or other youngsters so that we can pass our hunting heritage and our love and appreciation of God's creation on to them. If we don't, then it will be our fault if there is no hunting in the future.

Sure, you say, I agree with you, once my son or daughter is "old enough", I'll do it. Right now though, he or she wouldn't fit in with the rest of my hunting partners, would make too much noise, can't sit still or a variety of other reasons. But these aren't really reasons, they're just excuses! I've never heard an adult say, "the one thing I regret is that I spent too much time with my family."

If we want our children to enjoy and appreciate what we do, we need to instill the love of nature in them in their very early years. Show them pictures in your magazines, let them make their own wildlife scrapbook, take them on scouting trips, tell them stories at bedtime about your hunting and outdoor experiences, in short, MAKE THEM A PART OF YOUR EXPERIENCES!

If we wait until they are "old enough" they will have created their own form of entertainment and then it may be too late!

Even at three or four years of age they are old enough to take along on your non-hunting, camping and fishing expeditions. In fact at this age they are very eager to do such things. Don't dampen their enthusiasm and say "wait until you get bigger and then you can go."

You can show them deer tracks and trails, bedding locations, tree rubs and similar items you discover on your hikes. They will show you caterpillars, salamanders, grasshoppers, colored leaves and other items that their young inquisitive eyes discover along the way. REMEMBER, THERE IS NO SUCH AGE AS "NOT OLD ENOUGH."

The time for non-involvement is past. We must all get involved to preserve our hunting traditions for future generations. *Get involved in your own way, but get involved.*

Chapter 20

Gizmos, Gadgets, and Paraphernalia

Good Products and Misc. Equipment Information

This is a section devoted to products which I have used and which I feel are very *good* products. Outside of the binocular strap, which I developed and market myself, I have no interest or profit motive in any of these products. I just wanted to let you know about what I believe are some very good and useful products.

BATHING PRODUCTS: Good old fashioned baking soda works fine but there are several different companies which make scent eliminating products and soaps which you can use to bathe with and wash your clothes with. These products should use triclosan, which reduces or eliminates odor caused by human sweat.

BINOCULARS: Swarovski: For open country hunting I recommend the 10 x 50's and for brush hunting I would choose their 7 x 50's. Obviously there are a lot of other very good optics available, Leupold & Stevens being one of them, but these are what I use and I think that they are excellent and very comfortable to use. Swarovski Optic North America Limited One Wholesale Way Cranston, RI 02920

BINOCULARS AND SCOPE COVERS: Butler Creek: They make excellent flip up water proof covers for binoculars, scopes and cameras Butler Creek 290 Arden Dr. Belgrade Montana. 59714 The see-through covers are nice but the solid ones are more durable.

BINOCULAR AND CAMERA STRAPS: Neo Tech: They make an excellent strap which is flexible and shock absorbing and makes carrying heavy binoculars much easier. Neo Tech P.O. Box 429 Bozemann, Montana. 59715 or check your local camera store.

There are several binocular holders which are designed to keep your binoculars from flopping around, and if you hunt with binoculars you know how critical this is. I have developed one system which I find works extremely well for me and is very inexpensive and easily adjustable. If you are interested in purchasing my holder send me a check for $13.95 and I'll mail one to you. There are also several other binocular harnesses on the market. You can find information on them in Cabella's, Red Head, or other outdoor catalogues.

BORE CLEANER: Country Cover Co. Makes natural smelling bore cleaners and lubricants. This product is currently handled by Rete Richards, Cobleskill, N.Y. 12043 (1-800-282-5663). There are now a couple of other unscented gun oils which can be purchased from specialty stores.

BOOT DRESSING: Montana Pitch Blend all natural water resistant water dressing with no smelly silicone or chemical odor which can easily spook game animals. Good in any area which has pine trees. Check your local boot repair store.

CLOTHING: 1. Kathy Kelly Design 20080 S.W. Jaquith Rd., Newberg, Or. 97132 503-628-3695 Shirts, hats and specialty items.

2. Contain Hunting Clothes V.S.I. 690 Industrial Circle, Spokane, MN. 55379 (1-800-804-8588) Anti-bacterial fabric

3. Scent Lok. This company was the first to make charcoal impregnated clothes to be used for scent elimination in hunting situations. Several other companies have followed suit (pardon the pun) but this company was the first. Most major catalogues and sporting goods stores carry their products.

G.P.S. Units: I personally prefer to use a Trimble Scoutmaster because of some of the features it offers but there are several other good manufacturers out there. This is a very fast changing industry, typical of the electronics industry. Upgraded models and new and improved features are added continually.

GUN SLINGS: Safari Sling: Excellent light weight gun sling which allows you to carry the gun in the regular sling position over the shoulder. But more importantly, it allows you to carry the rifle when still hunting in the classic, at ready position in front of you. This sling also allows you to use your binoculars without having to put your rifle down and keeps your rifle ready at all times. Boonie Packer Products P.O. Box 12204 Salem, OR. 97309

HEARING AMPLIFIERS: For those of us who have suffered hearing damage for one reason or another, there are several products now on the market which will help you regain at least some of your hearing loss. I have tried several of these products. Stereo is better than mono as it allows you to locate the direction of the sound. Again check catalogues like Cabellas or Red Head. The amplifier which I use is made by Silver Creek Industries Box 1988 Monitowoc, WI 54221 (1-800-533-3277)

PACKS: There are numerous packs on the market, but one of my favorites is made by Packs Plus Co. They have several varieties of packs in all shapes and sizes. (1-541-688-3902)

RANGE FINDERS: My favorite is the 600 compact made by Bushnell. It is affordable and does a great job. Bushnell Corp. 9200 Cody Overland Park, KS. 66214

SCENT ELIMINATING PRODUCTS: B-Scent Free, Scent Shield by Robinson Laboratories, Scent-A-Way Hunter Specialties Inc., No Scent Spray and Scent Stopper Boot Creme by James Valley Scents. Carry these products in a small refillable atomizer. My favorite is B-Scent Free, which according to the manufacturers fights odor in three ways. It kills bacteria, prevents regeneration of new bacteria and even catches odorous gasses before they leave the body.

These products work chemically to eliminate human odor on your clothes, gloves and boots and in some cases neutralizes scent molecules which are released from your body. Use in high contact and high sweat areas.

SCOPES: Swarovski makes an excellent 3 x 9 variable which I use, which is very light weight and has amazing light gathering ability.

Swarovski One Wholesale Way, Cranston RI 02920 (1-800-426-3089)

Leupold & Stevens also makes some excellent variable scopes which cost less than those made by Swarovski. They call them their Vari-X III series and make them with four different magnifications. My choice would be the 2.5 x 8. Leupold & Stevens Inc. P.O. Box 688, Beaverton, OR 97075

SPOTTING SCOPES: Leupold & Stevens also make some excellent spotting scopes. They were one of, if not the first companies, to come up with high quality, small, compact spotting scopes. At this time I prefer their 12 x 40 variable. Leupold & Stevens Inc. P.O. Box 688, Beaverton, Oregon 97075.

SCOPE AND BINOCULAR CLEANERS: Leupold & Stevens make a great binocular and scope cleaning brush. Kleer Vu makes a great product which cleans and acts as an anti-fog and a anti-static agent. Kleer Vu 3005 N. 4th. East Idaho Falls, ID 83401

TAXIDERMISTS: Choose them with care. Pick one that you are familiar with or at least take a look at animals similar to yours which they have mounted to see how lifelike and alive they look. I use Adams Taxidermy located at 86784 Franklin Blvd. in Eugene, Oregon, and they have always done a very good job.

TRAIL TIMERS: There are several timers on the market. My favorite by far is the one produced by Non Typical Engineering, 2053 Schanock Drive, Green Bay, WI 54303 (1-800-527-0305) I like this system because it uses one main reader board and as many sensors as you want to purchase. This saves money and there is less chance of the units being stolen because they can be programmed so that they are of no use without the main reader board. This system can also be attached to a camera. Timers will save you hours and even days of research time.

TREE STANDS: Countless manufacturers now create an endless variety of tree stands. A person should have one lightweight scouting stand and if possible several other heavier, more comfortable portable stands. At this point my favorite stand is made and sold by Cabellas. This stand has a separate chain mounting bracket which the stand fits into. This allows you to climb the tree and secure the light weight mounting bracket and then install the heavier stand, once the bracket is securely attached. This also allows you to potentially have one or two tree stands and several mounting brackets, at various locations, so you can easily change your tree stand locations during the season or even on a day to day basis.

TREE STAND STEPS: Centaur Archery Inc. In my opinion these are the best tree steps that I've used and I've tried a lot of them. They're made out of aluminum, are very light weight and fold for easy, compact carrying. They can be used with multiple tree stand set ups as they are a two-part system made up of individual steps which can be attached to and removed from the permanent screws which are installed at your various tree stand locations. 12 to 14 steps and 40 or 50 screws should provide you with all of the tree stand locations you need. They are easy to install and remove and compact to carry. Centaur Archery Inc. 45 Hollinger Crescent #1 Kitchener, Ontario Canada N2K 2Z1 You can also purchase them from Cabellas.

THE FOLLOWING ARE ITEMS WHICH I CARRY INTO THE WOODS WITH ME WHEN I HUNT.

Survival gear enclosed in a water proof zippered pouch. This pouch contains extra flashlight, compass, knife, knife sharpener, string saw, rope, nylon twine, water proof matches, butane lighter, several fire starting materials, pitch impregnated dry wood chips, light plastic tarp, signalling mirror, and an aluminum space blanket. NEVER USE ANYTHING OUT OF THIS BAG EXCEPT IN AN EMERGENCY.

Quiet fanny or day pack. Binoculars. Compass. Range finder. Fawn bleat or distress call. Lens cleaning liquid, lens cleaning brush and lens cleaning tissue. Baking soda or one of the other scent eliminating products talked about in the book. Very small tape measure. Three extra bullets held together with rubber bands. (To date I've never had to use them) Clear butane lighter and dry wood chips. 99 cent cigarette pack sized, rain parka. Two disposable hand warmers. Binocular strap to keep my binoculars from flopping around when I'm walking or bending over to check sign. Camouflage cloth with ties on the end and a face mask or face paint.

Small 35 millimeter camera with two rolls of film enclosed in a zip lock baggie and a strap on or screw in miniature tripod.

Small battery operated headlight with extra batteries and bulb, to use when I'm walking out at night or packing out a deer late at night. I've found that the slightly larger four AA battery model is much more effective than the two AA battery models. A small but strong knife and a light weight folding saw and a medium weight nylon drag rope. This rope can be used to tie up the deer's legs while field dressing as well as helping drag out your deer. Make sure that the teeth of your folding saw cuts both wood and bone. Quiet waterproof gaiters to keep my lower legs dry. Wool covered, insulated, seat pad which attaches to my belt to use while still hunting, when I want to sit and watch an area or when I'm sitting in my tree stand. This protects me from moisture and ground chill. A warm hunter is a motionless quiet hunter. Florescent surveyors tape to use when I am learning the trails into a new area or used to mark the trail of a wounded deer. Be sure to remove the tape when you're done with it. Disposable rubber gloves and handi-wipes for dressing out game in dry weather and heavy duty zip lock bags for liver and heart.

Photo credit: Boyd Iverson

"Here's looking at you *II*."

I hope you enjoyed my book!

If you would like to order additional copies for yourself or for friends, please contact me for cost and shipping info.

If you would like to order the signed and numbered, hardbound, limited edition series, please contact me. There will only be 2,500 of these printed!

Mail any book orders, photos, or letters to:

Grassroots Publications
1872 Willamette St.
Eugene, Oregon 97401

Web site: www.efn.org/~iverson/trophy.shtml
E-mail: Iverson@efn.org